The Phonology Factor

Creating Balance with Beginning Readers

NADINE PEDRON
SUSAN BROWN

Pippin Publishing

Y8MDD / PED

Edited by Dyanne Rivers
Designed by John Zehethofer
Printed and bound in Canada by Friesens

Canadian Cataloguing in Publication Data

Pedron, Nadine
    The phonology factor: creating balance
    with beginning readers

(The Pippin teacher's library)
Includes bibliographical references.
ISBN 0-88751-084-1

1. Reading—Remedial teaching. 2. Reading—
Phonetic method. 3. English language—
Phonology. I. Brown, Susan. II. Title III. Series

LB1050.5.P42 1998   372.43   C98-932111-8

ISBN 088751-084-1

10   9   8   7   6   5   4   3   2   1

To our husbands, Gordon and Jeff,
for their support
throughout the writing of this book.

CONTENTS

. . . .

INTRODUCTION

Teachers who embrace literature-based, meaning-centered, whole language instruction have much to celebrate. The whole language approach — focusing the curriculum on the child and integrating language arts into all aspects of school programs — now pervades classrooms in many parts of the world. The use of relevant, functional reading and writing activities within a cooperative learning framework has made the construction of meaning a priority. In the process, children — and teachers — have discovered a new joy in and enthusiasm for language arts. What's more, whole language advocates have carried the flag promoting both the empowerment of teachers and the active participation of children in decision-making.

These are solid accomplishments, but there is still work to be done. Even in integrated language arts classrooms, some children are failing to learn to read. Why is this happening? The time has come for teachers to think seriously about this issue — and how we can provide even greater access to literacy to even greater numbers of children. We need to re-examine our assumptions based on our own observations of student learning and to reflect on this knowledge in light of current thinking in the field of early literacy.

That's what this book is about. Its first purpose is to examine the so-called reading wars — the continuing controversy that has pitted whole language supporters against phonics-first advocates — and assess the impact of recent research into the significance of phonological awareness on this controversy.

Its second purpose is to make the case for adopting a more eclectic approach that integrates direct, explicit instruction in phonological awareness into literature-based, meaning-centered programs. To accomplish this, we have included an in-depth description and explanation of phonological awareness and the important role it plays in helping children learn to read. A key element of this discussion is a summary of the research that supports including explicit phonological awareness instruction in the early grades. The intent is to meet the instructional needs of children who are at risk of failing to learn to read while sustaining the powerful principles of the whole language approach.

The final purpose of the book is to provide practical suggestions, based on current research, for assessment and instructional activities that promote phonological awareness in children in the emergent and beginning stages of literacy — five- to seven-year-olds and older learners with special needs. Assessing children's level of phonological awareness is a step that we believe is essential to both meeting the children where they are and planning where — with the teacher's help — they need to go next.

The suggested instructional activities are organized according to the stages at which phonological awareness appears to develop and are designed with both explicit instruction and integrated language arts in mind. They are intended both to meet the needs of students whose phonological awareness is not yet adequately developed and to reinforce the phonological skills of children whose awareness is more advanced.

These systematic and carefully sequenced activities are designed to be integrated seamlessly into whole language programs without disrupting or interfering with the naturalistic, communicative approach to learning that is the hallmark of these programs. Even activities geared specifically for teaching through direct instruction can be presented as mini-lessons — the essential instructional detours that have always been a vital component of the whole language approach.

Using This Book

At this stage, teachers who agree that phonological awareness is a critical element of the process of learning to read and write may be saying, "Yes, okay, but what do I do on Monday morning?"

The answer to this question lies in the assessment procedures and instructional activities that form the heart of this book.

Though we encourage you to read the research-based background information, we realize that you may be ready to move directly to the chapter that outlines instructional activities. Because these activities relate to the stages of phonological development, however, we urge you to start by assessing the children's level of phonological awareness. Tools for doing so are outlined in the chapter titled "Assessing Phonological Awareness."

Then, try a few activities that appear to meet the children's needs. With children who are at risk, try one or two of the suggested activities with an individual or a small group. Starting small — trying a few activities with a few children — will help you see and understand the concepts involved and evaluate their impact on the students.

As you learn more from your teaching and observation, your confidence will grow. We hope that you will find yourself using more and more of the suggestions, until you eventually feel comfortable creating activities of your own.

. . . .

THE BEST OF ALL WORLDS

Teaching children to read is one of the most challenging and rewarding responsibilities in the field of education. Yet the best way of doing this continues to be a hotly
debated educational issue.

The Roots of the Debate

During the first half of the 20th century, there was a tendency
to focus on easily observable aspects of behavior and to ignore
complex explanations of how children learn to read and write.
During this time, educators believed that both oral and written language consisted of separable components that included
phonology (the study of the sound systems of languages),
morphology and syntax (the study of word structures and
combinations), and semantics (the study of the meaning of
languages). This view resulted in teaching and testing prac-
tices that fragmented language into discrete, identifiable segments that could be easily assessed and taught. Little attention
was paid to the relationship among the components or to the
underlying purpose of the use of language. The communicative nature of language was ignored, and teaching methods
focused on drilling individual words and linguistic rules.

In the 1950s, though, controversy erupted as some educators started to question long-held assumptions about the effectiveness of the sight-word approach to teaching reading. In
his 1955 book, *Why Johnny Can't Read*, Rudolph Flesch advocated that phonics instruction replace the sight-word method-

ology that had prevailed since the 1930s. He argued that children from uneducated families entering school with little or no exposure to written language were at a disadvantage if they were not taught the alphabetic code.

Shortly afterwards, Samuel and Winifred Kirk responded with their article, "How Johnny Learns to Read." Refuting Flesch's theory, they argued that the sight-word approach was a far more valid instructional method. Neither argument acknowledged that learning to read involved any other processes.

While the view that language learning is a fragmented process prevailed in the mainstream, it was not universally accepted. John Dewey, for example, discussed the importance of integrating the curriculum, maintaining that all studies are related and all studies should relate school to real life. At the same time, New Zealanders Doris Lee and Lillian Lamoreaux wrote a book titled *Learning to Read through Experience*. In it, they introduced a teaching method called language experience, which advocates encouraging learners to express their personal experiences orally and in writing.

The Beginnings of Whole Language

The theoretical framework of language experience was a precursor of the whole language approach that began to take shape in the 1960s. As traditional views of reading instruction were challenged, language came to be viewed as an integrated system linked to cognition and influenced by motivation, learning, experience and emotion. Assessment and teaching were influenced by new developments in research that emphasized reading as communication. Teachers began to move away from focusing on letters and words to integrating language learning in naturalistic, communicative settings.

Whole language theory is based on the view that, because learning oral language is inherently integrative, a curriculum for teaching written language should be integrated as well. Whole language methods attempt to unify and integrate oral and written language and promote the construction of meaning through the use of materials and activities that have purpose for and relevance to the learner. It is believed that children develop literacy when they use it to perform functional, natural and authentic tasks that are meaningful and serve real purposes. As a result, advocates of the approach believe that children should be engaged in reading real literature and writing real text.

Underlying whole language principles is the belief that children are naturally predisposed to acquire written language in the same way as they acquire oral language. As a result, there is opposition to presenting the sub-skills of written language outside of meaningful literacy activities. In addition to this conviction about literacy, whole language advocates embrace the notion of a child-centered curriculum that is developmentally determined, encourage students to become independent learners, and believe that teachers should be empowered to make decisions about curriculum and instruction in their own classrooms.

The whole language movement enjoyed widespread acceptance during the 1980s and '90s. According to P. David Pearson, it "captured the rhetoric" of the language arts field, a fact that was reflected in changes in curricular approaches, publishers' offerings and teaching materials. He invited those who doubt this to examine the programs of the International Reading Association's national, state and local conferences and to scan the titles of articles appearing in popular language arts periodicals. Further evidence of its popularity may be found in the offerings of teacher-training courses and the professional development presentations sponsored by school boards and districts.

The Role of Phonics Instruction

At the same time as the whole language movement was growing and developing, research was continuing into the role of phonics in the reading process. Jeanne Chall's *Learning to Read: The Great Debate*, published in 1967, emphasized evidence pointing to the success of programs that stressed phonics instruction. Research conducted in the 1970s and '80s confirmed the benefits of including systematic phonics instruction in early reading. In 1985, the Center for the Study of Reading at the University of Illinois published *Becoming a Nation of Readers*, concluding that there was general agreement that phonics should be taught, but considerable disagreement over just how this should be done.

The consensus on the importance of phonics resulted from research that began in the early 1960s and reached fruition in the mid-1980s, when researchers such as Keith Stanovich, Anne E. Cunningham, Barbara Cramer and Dorothy Freeman found that children's level of phonological awareness — the explicit knowledge of the sound structure of language — is the best predictor of success in reading.

The Great Debate

This impressive research touched off fierce debate within the whole language community — and beyond. The current debaters cluster into two teams: whole language theorists and decoding methodologists. So fierce was the debate that a 1990 *Newsweek* article dubbed this controversy the reading wars.

Extending the *Newsweek* analogy, advocates of a parts-to-the-whole, sequential-skills, phonics-first approach can be described as troops in the bottom-up army, while advocates of a meaning-first, whole-to-the-parts, skills-will-naturally-emerge approach are members of the top-down army. The front-line soldiers in this war are the teachers who must implement the strategies decreed by the currently prevailing, often politically driven, camp.

Continuing the battlefield analogy, the extremists in both camps might be the warring generals — and perhaps the students caught in the theoretical crossfire are the casualties, a notion extended by Nancy Mather. In a 1992 article in *Learning Disabilities and Practice,* she wrote, "The exact number of losses, however, is rarely reported. In the interim, the peacemakers embrace whatever is usable and integrate new ideas and materials into an eclectic approach."

In fact, it appears that many experienced teachers know enough to duck the extreme swings of the educational pendulum. As new instructional models and methods are mandated, effective teachers seem to be able to incorporate and modify or expand them in order to continue providing what they believe works for the students in their classrooms. They find ways to provide balanced instruction no matter where the educational pendulum has currently come to rest.

The Best of All Worlds

Some whole language purists argue that any organized instruction in phonology violates whole language principles. They assert that direct instruction cannot be reconciled with natural learning and that activities that teach children to analyze language are irrelevant and without purpose. They further believe that skills should be taught only in context and when needed by children.

As the battle continues to rage, however, a growing number of researchers, theorists and policy-makers on both sides of the issue have become deeply concerned about the negative effects of this warfare on the field of reading. To focus energy on providing access to literacy for all students, they advocate the seeking of common ground — of finding points of agreement, reaching consensus, following a middle road, and embracing more eclectic approaches.

Marilyn Adams, for instance, embraces a skills-based philosophy, yet, in *Beginning to Read: Thinking and Learning about Print*, she stated, "We do, indeed, know a great deal about beginning reading. Yet the divisiveness over code-emphasis versus meaning-emphasis in reading instruction rages on. Isn't it time to stop bickering about which is more important? Isn't it time we recognized that written text has both form and function? To read, children must learn to deal with both, and we must help them."

In *Learning to Read: The Great Debate*, published in 1967, Jeanne Chall argued against both focusing exclusively on phonics instruction and teaching phonics in isolation. She agreed that children's literature rather than workbooks should be used, and that some teachers may overdo the use of phonics. And in a 1994 article in *The Reading Teacher*, Keith Stanovich suggested that whole language proponents might consider admitting that some children do not learn the alphabetic principle through simple immersion in print and that these children might benefit from explicit instruction in the alphabetic code.

Furthermore, authorities in the field of special education such as Benita Blachman and Nancy Mather recommend an eclectic approach that integrates phonological awareness activities into a classroom rich in oral and written language activities. With students who are learning disabled, Mather supports using the meaning-based, naturalistic curriculum of whole language programs, but also urges teachers to include explicit instruction in phonological awareness in order to accommodate the special needs of these children.

Marie Clay, the New Zealand developer of Reading Recovery, an effective early intervention program, contends that the more rigid a reading program, the more children will experience difficulty in learning to read. In her theoretical text, *Becoming Literate*, she suggested that about 80 percent of children will learn to read in most organized reading programs. If the program is highly prescribed and rigidly adhered to, however, the number of students who fail to learn to read will rise.

Clay stressed the complexity of the reading process and the need to recognize that different paths can lead to the same goal. While supporting the whole language approach, she believes that children who are struggling in whole language programs may not get enough direct and explicit instruction in sound-symbol relationships. Conversely, in classrooms that emphasize isolated phonics instruction, children may not be involved in enough literacy experiences to understand that making sense is what reading is all about. Clay advocated offering a balanced repertoire of reading strategies, providing explicit instruction for brief periods but placing the overriding emphasis on real reading and writing tasks.

In *Literacy at the Crossroads*, whole language advocate Regie Routman wrote that embracing a whole language approach does not rule out recognizing the importance of developing phonological awareness. She agreed that many teachers have not been adequately trained to skillfully use mini-focus lessons to highlight phonics skills. Arguing that whole language teachers must know how to teach explicitly and to provide demonstrations and directed lessons, she stated, "It becomes apparent that phonics and skills are part of whole language and always have been."

Courtney Cazden wrote *Whole Language Plus* in 1992 to promote her view that immersion in rich literacy environments is necessary, but not enough, to provide a complete literacy education. She asserted that students need help in focusing attention on specific features of written language; they need deliberate, well-planned help in attending to parts as well as wholes.

While Cazden is committed to many of the fundamental principles of whole language, she is also aware of its limitations, especially in the way it is sometimes practiced. Countering the notion that children can learn written language in the same way they do oral language, she argued that classrooms cannot replicate the kind of immersion in oral language that occurs in the home and that learning written symbols is a profoundly different enterprise from learning speech.

Cazden agreed that literacy learning can approximate oral-language learning in some ways, such as shared reading, the use of environmental print, reading children's books written in their natural language, and producing written language early on; however, she also maintained that, beyond these starting points, there is much to learn that requires active, systematic teaching.

What Do Teachers in Whole Language Classrooms Think?

The whole language movement inspired and re-energized teachers who had longed to use genuine literature in the early grades to integrate the curriculum, and to teach reading in a naturalistic way that appeals to teacher and student alike. Scores of teachers enthusiastically tell stories about exciting lessons, spontaneous reading, delightful creative writing, and thoroughly engaged students.

These same teachers, however, also voice concerns and raise thoughtful questions:

— Some of my students are still not learning to read.
— I am not clear about how to provide what the students need in phonics.
— Should I be using phonics instruction at all?
— What do I need to consider for learners who are at risk? What do they need to succeed?

Questions raised by thoughtful teachers about the effectiveness of their programs, the students who are struggling, and the role of phonics also indicate a growing awareness of and receptivity to more systematic, planned and explicit instructional techniques. They believe that phonics instruction can be compatible with whole language — and that including instruction in specific skills and strategies helps develop a more powerful tool for educating children.

In fact, they argue that if whole language does not include systematic instruction in the alphabetic code and analyzing language (metalinguistics), it fails to live up to its claim to support students' efforts to become proficient in all aspects of language. While they believe in the meaning-based integrated nature of whole language, they also believe that this is incomplete without direct instruction in metalinguistic skills.

Which Students Need More Explicit Teaching?

Several groups of children cause teachers concern:

— Those who have language-learning problems.
— Those who have not experienced a literacy-rich home environment.
— Those who are learning English as a second language.
— Other children, not as easily identified, who simply come to the reading task with more than the usual degree of confusion about the reading process.

LANGUAGE LEARNING PROBLEMS

These children demonstrate a delay in or disorder of their oral language development, often characterized by a limited range of oral language structures and vocabulary, as well as errors in articulating speech and difficulty retrieving words. Interestingly, it appears that a common problem area for many of these children is in phonological processing — developing phonological awareness.

To understand why these children may not succeed in whole language classrooms, it is important to look at the theory underlying whole language methodology. The construct upon which the whole language movement is based — that literacy is acquired in the same manner as oral language is learned — appears to be valid as well as appealing. If we accept this assumption, we would expect whole language methodology to be effective with students who have acquired language in a normal developmental way; that is, with students who have learned speech and language skills and rules without explicit instruction. For most children, learning oral language is a naturally evolving process. They seem to learn to understand and use language effortlessly. By the time they are ready to start school, they have at their command most of the phonological, grammatical and syntactical structures of language.

For some children, however, language skills have not developed so easily. These are the pre-schoolers and children in the early grades who need extra help — more focused, repetitive and explicit language experiences — in order to be able to extract and apply the rules that govern speech and oral language. Many of these children also need more focused, repetitive and explicit instruction to achieve success in early literacy.

Our experiences with students who have language-learning problems have convinced those of us who teach them that whole language classrooms provide the rich, meaning-centered learning environment that these students need. As more of these children become involved in the full-inclusion special education model, this environment is more accessible to them. However, we also strongly argue that, in addition to — and within — the natural communicative environment of a whole language classroom, these children need activities that include explicit and sequential instruction.

While the terms "learning disabled" and "dyslexic" are often used to describe students who have trouble learning to read and write, the definitions of these terms vary and offer little guidance for developing a teaching methodology. Labels like these may, in fact, inhibit acceptance of these children and lower teachers' academic expectations of them.

We prefer to describe children who are struggling to meet the demands of early literacy activities as "at risk," and it is this term that is used throughout this book. Most early literacy teachers have in their classes a few children who require more explicit teaching as a result of language-learning issues, in particular those connected to phonological awareness.

LACK OF EARLY LITERACY EXPERIENCES

Children who have been exposed to a rich variety of literacy activities at home — being read to, discussing stories and print conventions, chanting nursery rhymes, and playing with language — have had many opportunities to develop phonological awareness before they enter school. Not all children in our classrooms have been exposed to literacy experiences or materials at home, however. For those who haven't, it is essential for the school to provide these experiences.

ENGLISH-AS-A-SECOND-LANGUAGE LEARNERS

Many children whose home language is not English have not been immersed since babyhood in experiences with English, though they may have had plenty of language experiences in their home language. These students need many and varied oral language experiences and instructional texts appropriate to their level of English proficiency. In addition, assessing their stage of phonological awareness in English is important.

Do Children Need Explicit Instruction in Phonological Awareness?

Clearly, some children fail to learn to read in whole language classrooms.

Recent research suggests that phonological awareness correlates directly to reading ability. It is postulated that the poor decoding skills of unsuccessful readers relate to low phonological awareness and result in an inability to isolate, analyze and synthesize the sounds — phonemes — that make up language. Longitudinal studies indicate that students who demonstrate poor phonemic awareness skills when they enter school continue to experience difficulty throughout their school careers. It appears to be critical, then, to assess and monitor the phonological awareness of students in the early stages of reading instruction and to provide explicit instruction to those who need it. A more detailed discussion of the specific research that points to this conclusion is set out in the chapter titled "What the Research Tells Us."

The guidelines, suggestions and activities outlined in this book are based on the assumption that explicit instruction in phonological awareness can be integrated into a whole language approach — and that this kind of eclectic approach is, in fact, the most powerful model of reading instruction.

. . . .

WHAT IS

PHONOLOGICAL AWARENESS?

Communication in our society involves speaking, listening, reading and writing. The ability to speak and listen precedes the ability to read and write, and the strength of children's oral language system often determines the degree of success they will experience in early literacy programs. Fortunately, the field of language development is heavily researched and, as linguists continue this research, educators continue to find ways to link this knowledge to classroom instruction.

International research shows that language is a rule-governed communication system and that young children the world over learn language in much the same way, in the same sequence of developmental stages, and for similar reasons. While various theories have been put forward to explain just how we learn to use oral language, there is general agreement that babies come into the world biologically programmed to do so if they have other humans to communicate with. Most children require no direct instruction from adults to learn the rules of speech and language structure. Because they are driven by their need to communicate, their utterances are meaningful, purposeful and subject to continual refinement until they use language that reflects what they hear in their environment.

Some exceptions to this rule occur when adults teach children the verbal niceties — the social expressions that parents believe are important to their child's cultural survival and acceptability. For example, early in their language development, children are often explicitly taught "please" and "thank-you" routines because they do not naturally recognize these as meaningful or communicative.

What Is Phonological Awareness?

Linguists identify five components of language:

— Phonology: The study of the sounds (phonemes) that comprise a language.
— Semantics: The study of the meaning of language (words, phrases and other connected units).
— Morphology: The study of word structure (e.g., altering root words to form verb inflections, plurals, possessives, etc.).
— Syntax: The study of word combinations and sentence structure.
— Pragmatics: The study of the social use of language (how people adjust their use of language to reflect the demands and expectations of various communication situations).

Phonology is the component addressed in this book. If phonology is the study of the sounds (phonemes) that comprise a language, phonological awareness is the awareness of the sounds that make up words.

Though our written language system is based on our oral language system, it is not biologically imprinted as is oral language. As a result, the ability to read and write must be taught. While the links between spoken and written language are widely recognized by theorists, the connections between the two are complex and require careful study.

In some languages, such as Spanish and Italian, there is nearly always a direct correspondence between a phoneme — the smallest unit of sound — and the letter, or grapheme, that represents it. This correspondence isn't as clear in English, however. While there are 26 letters in the English alphabet, there are, generally speaking, 37 phonemes. A phoneme can be represented by a single letter, such as S, or a combination of two letters such as SH or TH. Furthermore, English is confusing because a letter may represent more than one phoneme (e.g., C as in "city" and as in "cat"). When educators talk about graphophonic sources of information, they are referring to this sound-letter representation.

When babies babble, they are practicing the production of the sounds of a language. In the earliest stages of babbling, they are capable of producing every sound or phoneme of every language. As they grow older, however, they begin to reflect the language they hear around them and limit their production to the sounds heard in their environment.

In every language, rules govern which phonemes can be combined and in what order. Young children learn these rules without direct instruction. As their speech develops, they begin to combine phonemes in a specific order to articulate words. At first, these may be incomplete or misarticulated imitations of the word but, in most cases, they eventually become entirely intelligible. Although they are able to combine various phonemes into words, young children perceive speech as a continuous flow, making no distinction between word boundaries. The ability to make this distinction is a skill that must be learned.

Although the ability to efficiently use the phonological component of oral language — to produce speech sounds clearly and appropriately when talking — is desirable and helpful, it does not guarantee that children who possess it will develop the phonological awareness needed to learn to read and write. In fact, in order to read and write English, children must learn the concept of word and letter. They must understand that a spoken word matches a printed word and how to divide a word into discrete sounds and groups of sounds. They must understand that words are made up of sounds arranged from left to right. In addition, they must develop their metalinguistic skill — the ability to think about and analyze their own language.

Speech is fluid, phrased, rhythmic and heedless of the boundaries between words. In fact, in languages that do not have a written form, there is no word for word! Take the word "cat," for example. In natural speech, it is not divided into separate sounds, but is uttered as a single syllable that often merges with the pronunciation of an adjoining word or words. To read or write "cat," a child who can hear, understand and say the word must learn that it is a one-syllable word made up of three separate sounds, with a beginning sound (onset) /k/ and an ending cluster of sounds (rime) /æt/.

Because oral language is not naturally segmented into sounds, it is not surprising that children must be taught to match their speech to print and that some children have considerable difficulty doing so. Learning to read in English requires that they learn an alphabetic system, which means that they must learn the letter sounds as discrete units.

When trying to read an unknown word, though, proficient readers rarely sound out each separate sound. Rather, they tend to draw on their knowledge of syllables and onset and rime patterns to make comparisons to words and chunks of words they already know. The ability to recognize that written language is segmented into words, syllables and letters is critical to learning to read and write successfully — and some children are unable to do this without explicit instruction.

In English, the sounds within words are distinguished in three ways:

— By syllables.
— By onsets and rimes (e.g., in the word "cat," /k/ is the onset and /æt/ is the rime).
— By phonemes (letter sounds).

A child's level of phonological awareness is measured by the degree to which she or he can manipulate and reflect on the arrangement of the sounds in oral language. Research tells us that syllables are easier to hear than the sounds of individual letters and that the ability to distinguish the individual sounds in words develops later than the ability to identify syllables. Most children have little trouble dividing words into syllables but find dividing words and syllables into phonemes more demanding because, in connected speech, phonemes are abstract units that are combined fluidly to form words. Furthermore, phonemes usually carry no meaning, and because children are accustomed to thinking about language in terms of meaning, they have no reason to identify individual sounds for the purposes of communicating orally.

Children whose phonological awareness is well-developed can examine language independently of meaning, divide words into phonemes and manipulate these. They can, for example, identify the three sounds in "fish" and blend the separately articulated sounds — /f//ɪ/ʃ/ — to create the word "fish." They can also create new words by deleting or substituting sounds (e.g., /d/ for /f/ in "fish" to make the word "dish"). This ability requires them to manipulate onsets and rimes. Understanding the concept of onset and rime enables a child to create word families (e.g., cat, sat, pat, etc.) and use the principle of analogy to read new words. For example, a child who encounters "that" for the first time may use her knowledge of the rime /æt/ in "cat" to read the new word.

To understand more clearly what phonological awareness skills are, it may help to examine examples of assessment tasks that are sometimes used to determine a child's level of awareness. More detailed assessment procedures are described in the chapter titled "Assessing Phonological Awareness."

— Deleting phonemes: What would be left if the /t/ sound were left out of "cat"? What sound do you hear in "cat" that is missing in "at"?
— Word-to-word matching: Do "cat" and "cook" begin with the same sound?
— Blending: What word would we have if we put these sounds together — /k//æ//t/?
— Isolating sounds: What is the first sound in "cat"?
— Segmenting phonemes: What sounds do you hear in the word "cat"?
— Identifying the odd word out: Which of these words starts with a different sound from the others — "dog," "done," "cat," "dime"?
— Sound-to-word matching: Is there a /t/ in "cat"?
— Identifying onset and rime: What sounds do "sat" and "cat" have in common?

Successful readers seem to develop phonemic awareness — awareness of the distinct and separate sounds in words — at the same time as they develop word-recognition skills, while children who fail to learn to read don't. In fact, phonemic awareness may be the single most powerful determiner of success in reading — and some children require explicit and systematic instruction to develop it.

What about Phonics?

Where does phonics fit into this picture?

Phonics has come to mean the activities, programs and instructional sequences that we provide to students in classrooms to help them learn how to link a sound to a letter or letters, to blend them into words, and to decode unknown words by "sounding them out." Traditionally, phonics has been taught by teaching a letter, then the sound that corresponds to that letter. In English, this task is complicated because the correspondence between letters and sounds is inconsistent. Commercial publishers have produced scores of instructional programs designed to help teach phonics to children in the early grades. As a result, teaching phonics has come to be equated with workbook drills that are unconnected to real literature.

As outlined in the chapter titled "The Best of All Worlds," the whole language movement has eschewed this kind of traditional phonics instruction, maintaining that it is inconsistent with the way children learn oral language. Traditional educators, on the other hand, insist that phonics be taught in systematic and explicit formats. While the two sides agree that a knowledge of phonics is necessary for learning to read and write, debate continues to swirl around when, how — and how much — phonics should be taught.

The primary intent of teaching phonics is to provide a tool to help children decode new text. Traditional phonics programs with a predetermined sequence of instruction have failed to help — and, worse, confused — many children. Perhaps this is because these children did not know that words comprise a sequence of sounds; they had not yet achieved a sophisticated level of phonological awareness.

What would happen, for instance, if a teacher said to Susie, "The letter M makes the sound that you hear at the beginning of 'mother.'" If Susie does not understand the concept of word and that words are made up of sounds, she wouldn't have a clue about what the teacher meant. At this point, she would not benefit from instruction in phonics.

Furthermore, if Susie were exposed to a phonics program that taught rules, she might be able to recite the rules and even say, "The letter M makes the /m/ sound," but she would not be able to use this information to write or sound out a printed word until she could hear and isolate the /m/ sound in a word. A child like Susie first needs to learn how to segment the words and sounds of oral language.

Phonics-first traditionalists believe that there should be explicit instruction in phonics, while whole language purists believe that it should be taught implicitly, within the context of meaningful reading and writing tasks. When taught explicitly, children are instructed in the sounds represented by individual letters (e.g., the letter M says /m/, as in the word "mother"). When instruction is implicit, the sounds are not produced in isolation. A child is expected to discover the sounds made by letters as a result of hearing and reading words in stories and lists (e.g., after reading the words "man," "milk," "money" and "mother," a child is expected to induce that the letter M says /m/). A child who came upon an unknown word would be asked to think of another word that starts like "mother" and apply the /m/ sound to the new word. To do this, she must be able to distinguish the initial sound, something that is difficult because of the fluidity of spoken language. For the child who is unable to segment words into discrete sounds, this task is impossible.

Furthermore, explicit instruction in phonics is complicated by the complex nature of English. Some consonant sounds, such as those made with a brief explosion of air — the "plosives" B, D, G, J, K, P and T — become distorted when isolated (e.g., B becomes "buh"). In addition, blending sounds is essential to phonics instruction, but blending often presents a problem in traditional programs, leaving many children unable to apply what they have learned about letter-sound correspondences to the task of decoding words in text.

This book stresses the importance of using writing to learn how to hear, distinguish, separate and make links between sounds and letters. Learning through writing, a process that links sound to letter, known to unknown, and oral language to written language, provides the beginning support that children need to recognize that words can be divided into sounds. In addition, the book focuses on activities that encourage children to recognize chunks or groups of letters and letter patterns in unknown words, and to use a known word to decode an unknown word.

Strategies such as these often enable children to bypass the stumbling block presented by the necessity of learning to blend separate sounds. In the Reading Recovery program, which works successfully with the lowest-achieving beginning readers, blending is not taught in the traditional way. Much of what we offer in our activities section is directly linked to the principles of Reading Recovery.

26

. . . .

WHAT THE RESEARCH

TELLS US

The research into phonological awareness has significantly influenced current thinking in the field of reading and, in particular, whole language. Because the assessment and instructional activities presented in this book have been informed and influenced by this research, it is critical to understand the rationale behind them. Furthermore, understanding this rationale will enable you to generate your own activities, rather than relying only on those included in this book.

Phonological Awareness and Reading Success

Early studies investigated the developmental aspects of phonological awareness and its relationship to early literacy. Later research has explored the effectiveness of explicit training in phonological awareness in helping children learn to read and write. These studies have established that children's level of phonological awareness is not only one of the best predictors of the degree of success they are likely to experience in learning to read, but also plays a causal role in learning to read.

The research reviewed in this chapter asked two fundamental questions:

— Can children be trained to analyze and segment phonological information?
— Does specific instruction in phonological awareness improve a child's ability to read and write?

One notably successful model was developed by the psychologist D.B. Elkonin in 1973. He believed that children should hear and learn to segment sound sequences in words before being introduced to print. To train children in this skill, he provided a picture of an object. Below the picture, he placed a rectangle divided into squares representing the exact number of phonemes in the name of the pictured object. A child was given markers (counters, chips, etc.) and asked to slowly articulate the word representing the object and to place a marker representing each sound in the appropriate square under the picture. Elkonin found that this physical manipulation of a visual representation helps the child learn to recognize the discrete sounds in words. Later, the child stops requiring markers and, once he knows how to form letters, can be asked to print the corresponding letters.

Five- and six-year-olds trained in Elkonin's technique were more successful at dividing words into their phonemic components than those who weren't. The procedure has been adapted for use with six- and seven-year-olds in the Reading Recovery early intervention program and will be further described in the activities section of this book.

In 1976, Michael and Lise Wallach conducted another study that found that children read more proficiently after being taught about phonemes. The six- and seven-year-olds who were taught to divide words into onset and rime and phonemes, then blend the sounds orally, scored significantly higher than those in the control group when their ability to read lists of words, as well as some prose, was tested.

And, in 1983, Lynette Bradley and Peter Bryant claimed that they had established a causal relationship between phonological awareness and reading when they measured the ability of four- and five-year-old non-readers to categorize sounds. Tasks consisted of picking the odd word out of a list of words such as "bun," "run," "hut" and "sun." As the researchers expected, there was a high degree of correlation between children's ability to categorize sounds and their level of reading proficiency when tested more than three years later. The causal relationship was demonstrated when some of the children with low initial scores on the categorization tasks participated in three years of training in phonological analysis. The control groups, which received no training in phonological analysis, included children whose initial scores were also low. At the end of the three-year period, the reading and spelling scores of the groups that received the phonological training significantly surpassed those of the control groups.

Bradley and Bryant found that the most effective training technique involved using plastic letters to show the children how sounds are represented by the letters of the alphabet, which suggests that training in categorizing sounds is more effective when it also involves an explicit connection with the alphabet. This study has come to be recognized as strong support for the hypothesis that an awareness of the sounds within words powerfully influences the level of success children will experience when learning to read and spell.

Another frequently cited longitudinal study was conducted by Ingvar Lundberg, Jorgen Frost and Ole-Peter Peterson in Denmark, where children enter school at the age of seven. The study, published in 1988, followed about 400 children from pre-school until they were eight, and evaluated a training program consisting of metalinguistic games and exercises intended to stimulate the children to discover and attend to the phonological structure of language. The researchers wanted to determine whether phonological awareness can be developed through training before formal reading instruction starts, whether the effects of early training are lasting, and whether the training helps children learn to read and spell in school.

The study found that children who received the pre-school training in phonological awareness read and spelled better by the time they were eight than those who did not. As a result of this analysis, the researchers concluded that early phonological awareness training provides a strong foundation for future success at reading and spelling.

In studies conducted in the late 1980s, Connie Juel also found that developing phonemic awareness early in their school careers was critical to children's successfully learning to read and write.

These are only a few of the studies that indicate that phonological awareness and knowledge of the alphabet are the top predictors of the degree of reading success that will be experienced by six- and seven-year-olds. In addition, several experimental studies indicate that early training in phonological awareness also promotes later success in reading and spelling.

What Kind of Training Is Most Effective?

A number of studies have found that children who are trained to recognize letter-sound correspondences, at either the phoneme or the onset-rime level, score higher on word-reading tests than those who are trained to recognize whole words. In addition, other studies have found that children who were trained in phoneme awareness *and* to recognize letter sounds significantly outperformed children whose language experiences consisted of listening to stories, lessons in vocabulary development, and instruction in the sounds of letters. Researchers concluded that it is the combination of phoneme awareness instruction and letter-sound knowledge that has the most marked beneficial effect on early literacy acquisition.

In the field of education, there is a growing awareness that writing and reading are reciprocal processes, and that writing may play an important role in helping children develop phonological awareness. Perhaps this is because writing is a segmentation task requiring a child to slowly say the sounds in a word in order to write the corresponding letter.

Marie Clay believes that children learn these segmentation skills best in the context of real reading and writing tasks. In *Becoming Literate*, she wrote, "My assumption is that the reader/writer can most easily become articulate about phonological aspects of reading when he is already making use of them, that is, once he is reading and writing small stretches of text." This is good news for whole language teachers! Clay's preference for learning about the phonological aspects of reading during real reading and writing is reflected in many of the suggestions and activities presented later in this book.

It's worth noting that some research also indicates that the level of structure used by the teacher when presenting instructional activities designed to develop phonological awareness is a critical variable. A 1983 study by Ake Olofsson and Ingvar Lundberg found that children exposed to highly structured training — three or four carefully planned, well-organized, 15- to 30-minute lessons a week — showed the most progress. In contrast, children exposed to the least structured activities — teachable moments provided incidentally and spontaneously — made no progress. These results support the theory that phonological awareness develops most effectively through lessons that are carefully planned and structured.

Can the Research Findings Be Applied in the Classroom?

The world of a tightly controlled research study is often very different from the real world of a classroom full of flesh-and-blood five-, six- or seven-year-olds. Can the training in phonological awareness that has been so successful in research studies be effectively duplicated by classroom teachers?

In 1991, Benita Blachman and other researchers decided to seek an answer to this question. To do so, they conducted a study among five- and six-year-olds in four demographically comparable, low-income, inner-city schools in upstate New York. Because all the schools reported a high incidence of reading failure, the study was able to evaluate not only a classroom model of phonological awareness training, but also its effectiveness in schools in which reading achievement was a major concern.

Lessons for the children who received phonological awareness training included work with manipulatives to learn sound segmentation, other segmentation-related activities, and instruction in letters and sounds. The children in the control group received no special training, though they continued to participate in the traditional classroom curriculum that included whole-class instruction in letter names and sounds.

The study found that the group that received the special training scored significantly higher than the control group in phonological awareness, letter-sound knowledge, and the ability to read words and non-words and produce invented spellings. Of interest is the fact that previous research studies had pointed to a positive correlation between a child's ability to produce invented spellings and early reading achievement. Data collected for the Blachman study support the theory that phonological awareness training that includes instruction in sound-symbol correspondences results in a higher level of invented spelling. Most important, though, the researchers concluded that classroom teachers can incorporate these activities into the regular school day and that the training has a positive effect on important beginning reading and spelling skills.

A similar study conducted by Rollanda O'Conner in 1996 found that teachers of five- and six-year-olds can provide phonological awareness activities in their classrooms without requiring any changes in class size, makeup or the level of additional assistance needed. By introducing activities that fit into their regular classroom routines, teachers were able to improve the phonological skills of the children.

Clearly, substantial evidence supports the wisdom of including phonological awareness training in classrooms. The apparent positive link between phonological awareness training and early literacy acquisition has convinced many educators that this training is an important aspect of classroom instruction.

Is Phonological Awareness Instruction Needed in Whole Language Classrooms?

Some educators argue that beginning readers do not need to be explicitly taught phonological awareness because they will acquire it naturally in classrooms using whole language, meaning-based approaches and a wide variety of good literature. They postulate that readers gain this knowledge as they encounter a rich array of print with a teacher who skillfully facilitates their learning by presenting authentic reading and writing activities.

Others maintain that while some types of phonological awareness, such as non-analytical rhyme and alliteration knowledge, are acquired naturally through exposure to literature in the pre-school years, *explicit* phonemic awareness — the analytical ability that enables children to segment and manipulate the phonemes in words — requires knowledge of the alphabetic system and may require direct and specific instruction. In *Becoming Literate*, Marie Clay wrote, "(The sources of phonological awareness) lie in oral language but not in a form needed by the reader. Individuals may vary remarkably in the degree to which letter-sound relationships, simple or complex, are induced without specific instruction as they learn to read."

As a result of a study they conducted in 1993, Joanna Uhry and Margaret Jo Shepherd of Columbia University Teachers College believe that the most important factor contributing to their positive outcomes may have been the *combination* of explicit instruction in segmentation and spelling with the meaningful writing experiences that take place in whole language classrooms.

Still, the question remains: Do children learn to segment phonemes in words in a whole language classroom in which phonemic awareness and knowledge of the alphabet are not directly taught?

Although some children are certainly able to develop phonological awareness as a result of rich exposure to language and literature, many others have trouble distinguishing the phonemes in words and learning which letters represent those phonemes without explicit instruction. This kind of explicit instruction is particularly critical for children who are at risk of failing to learn to read proficiently. The research in this area documents that deficiencies in phonological awareness underlie many of the difficulties experienced by these readers and that teaching them phonological awareness skills significantly improves their reading proficiency.

Although current research strongly supports including phonological awareness instruction in early literacy classrooms, integrating this instruction into whole language classrooms without violating — in the view of some educators, at least — the tenets of whole language theory has proven difficult. Authorities in reading recognize the value of rich and varied oral and written language activities inherent in whole language, meaning-based reading programs. Fortunately, some children are able to perceive and analyze the internal structure of words on their own; other children, however, need structured and explicit instruction in phonological awareness in order to successfully learn about the structure of words.

. . . .

ASSESSING

PHONOLOGICAL AWARENESS

Phonological awareness is not an all-or-nothing trait, something a person either does or does not possess. Rather, the development of this awareness proceeds in stages, reflecting an increasing ability to recognize that speech is made up of discrete items that can be manipulated. In order to plan appropriate instruction in phonological awareness or phonics, teachers need assessment tools that provide information about the development of each child.

Various assessment instruments have been developed to help determine children's awareness of and ability to segment and manipulate units of oral and written language. These can be used to plan instructional activities and to identify children who may need specific early intervention in order to learn to read and write successfully.

A word of caution is in order, however. Tasks developed for assessment purposes do not necessarily make appropriate instructional tools. Simply structuring instructional tasks that resemble the assessment tasks described in this chapter may not help children learn the concepts. In addition, successfully completing an assessment task does not necessarily ensure that a child will learn to read successfully. On the other hand, the inability to complete these tasks does not necessarily mean that the child cannot use phonological awareness skills to read successfully.

In assessing a child's level of phonological awareness, you may wish to use a formal, researched and validated assessment instrument that provides normative data enabling you to compare students to others or informal assessments that may yield more information for teaching purposes or both. Examples of both kinds of assessment tools are provided in this chapter, along with comments about their usefulness based on our experiences with children and teachers.

Formal Assessment

In addition to the Yopp-Singer test described in the following material, we have found that the spelling-by-stage assessment set out by Donald Bear and others in *Words Their Way* and the dictation sub-task set out by Marie Clay in *An Observation Survey* are very useful. Teachers who are familiar with the developmental stages of children's writing, however, can achieve much the same results by analyzing children's writing samples, an informal tool described later in this chapter.

YOPP-SINGER TEST

In 1988, Hallie Yopp conducted a study to investigate the validity and reliability of phonemic awareness tests. Using this preliminary work, she then developed, refined and validated the Yopp-Singer Test of Phoneme Segmentation. The test is made up of 22 words selected on the basis of word familiarity and feature analysis. The test is administered to individual children and takes about five to 10 minutes to complete. A child's score is based on the number of items that are correctly segmented into all phonemes.

Yopp found that the five- and six-year-old subjects of her study displayed a wide range of performance on the sample used to develop the test. For those assessed in the second semester of their first year of school, mean scores were approximately 11 out of 22 correct. Yopp suggested that children who get all or almost all the items correct can be considered phonemically aware, while students who get some items correct demonstrate an emerging awareness. Those who can segment only a few words — or none at all — lack phonemic awareness. A copy of the test is provided on the following page.

Analysis

While this assessment tool provides valuable information about whether a child can accurately divide words into pho-

YOPP-SINGER TEST OF PHONEME SEGMENTATION

Student's Name _____

Date _____

Score (number correct) _____

Directions: Today we're going to play a word game. I'm going to say a word and I want you to break the word apart. You are going to tell me each sound in the word in order. For example, If I say "old," you should say /o/-/l/-/d/. (*Administrator*: Be sure to say the sounds, not the letters, in the word.) Let's try a few together.

Practice items: ride, go, man (Help the child segment these items as necessary.)

Test items: Circle those items that the child correctly segments. Incorrect responses may be recorded on the blank line following the item.

1.	dog	_____	12.	lay	_____
2.	keep	_____	13.	race	_____
3.	fine	_____	14.	zoo	_____
4.	no	_____	15.	three	_____
5.	she	_____	16.	job	_____
6.	wave	_____	17.	in	_____
7.	grew	_____	18.	ice	_____
8.	that	_____	19.	at	_____
9.	red	_____	20.	top	_____
10.	me	_____	21.	by	_____
11.	sat	_____	22.	do	_____

The author, Hallie Kay Yopp, California State University, Fullerton, grants permission for this test to be reproduced. The author acknowledges the contribution of the late Harry Singer to the development of the test, which first appeared in *The Reading Teacher* (Vol. 49, no. 1: September 1995).

nemes, it does not tell teachers where children are in the earlier developmental stages of phonological awareness. This knowledge is essential for teachers who wish to scaffold children's learning from a particular stage of development.

Some children may not yet have internalized the concept of segmenting words in the flow of continuous speech, or understand that a spoken word matches a printed word, or even be able to distinguish letters, sounds and words. Because assessment often drives instruction, a teacher might assume that a child who cannot segment phonemes on the Yopp test should be provided with activities similar to the tasks in the assessment. For some children, this kind of instructional activity may be ineffective and confusing, leading to frustration.

Informal Assessments

ANALYZING WRITING SAMPLES

Because children are encouraged to use invented spellings in whole language classrooms, teachers have access to many examples of their writing. Examining these can provide insight into their knowledge of how language is mapped into print and what they know about phoneme segmentation and how sounds are represented in print.

The research on phonemic awareness and the development of the ability to spell has yielded information on the stages of spelling that has been used to develop various spelling inventories. A knowledge of the developmental stages can help teachers analyze children's writing to determine the stage they are at and provide direction for helping them move toward the next stage.

Examining the writing samples of individual children and using this examination to fill out the developmental spelling stages checklist on the following pages will help you analyze and document their stage of development.

OBSERVING PHONOLOGICAL AWARENESS

This informal assessment of the aspects of phonological awareness that are essential to learning to read is designed to be used with individuals or small groups. It includes six tasks,

Name _____

I. PRE-LITERATE AND PRE-PHONEMIC —
   Early Message Writing

1. Drawing

   _____

2. Random marks on page,
   formless scribbling

   _____

3. Repetitive forms

   _____

4. Scribbling in conventional direction

   _____

5. Letter-like forms

   _____

6. Pretend writing using known letters

   _____

II. EARLY PHONEMIC —
    Letter Name

7. Writes salient sounds of a word or syllable
   (e.g., b for bus, p for stop)

   _____

8. Uses most beginning
   and ending consonants
   (e.g., gt for get, bg for big)

   _____

III. LETTER NAME

9. Uses a vowel in most syllables,
   continues to use letter name
   for some short vowels
   (e.g., set for sit, pat for pet)   _____

10. Spells regular short vowel patterns correctly
    (e.g., big, cat, red)   _____

11. Uses most consonant blends
    and digraphs correctly
    (e.g., ch, th, tr)   _____

IV. TRANSITIONAL

12. Uses many features
    of conventional spelling   _____

13. Uses but confuses some long vowels
    (e.g., trane for train, hiev for hive)   _____

14. Correctly spells most single-syllable words
    with long vowels   _____

15. Uses "ed" and other
    grammatical inflections   _____

16. Spells endings phonetically
    (e.g., tradishun for tradition)   _____

17. Correctly spells unusual blends and digraphs
    (e.g., fought)   _____

18. Doubles consonants appropriately
    (e.g., stopping, better)   _____

19. Uses plurals correctly   _____

20. Uses prefixes and suffixes correctly   _____

21. Understands and uses derived spellings
    (e.g., explaination for explanation)   _____

V. CONVENTIONAL

22. Uses correct spellings   _____

organized in sequence from the easiest to the most complex, that answer six questions:

— Can the child clap the syllables of words he knows well?
— Can the child clap each word she hears in a simple sentence that includes only words that carry meaning?
— Can the child clap each word he hears in a more complex sentence that includes prepositions and articles?
— Can the child match a spoken word to a printed word in text?
— Can the child recognize words that rhyme and identify the onsets and rimes?
— Can the child divide one-syllable words into their component phonemes?

As each activity is presented, its importance to reading instruction is discussed, guidelines for observing the children are described, and links to instructional activities provided in the chapter titled "Instructional Activities" are suggested.

The assessment activities require little preparation or materials, and each takes between five and 10 minutes to complete. The information gathered can be applied directly to instructional planning for individual children or small groups. Sample sheets for keeping individual and class records are included at the end of this chapter.

Clapping Syllables

WHAT WE WANT TO KNOW: Can the child clap the syllables in words he knows well?

WHY WE WANT TO KNOW: An ability to segment the units of oral language is necessary to learning to read proficiently. Hearing chunks of sound is easier than hearing single sounds within words. Hearing and recognizing syllables is easier for children than distinguishing words in a sentence. This is a good first step in the phonemic segmentation task.

WHAT TO DO: Choose the names of one or two children in the group and model the clapping of the syllables in these names. With the children, say the names of others in the group. Ask the children to clap the syllables in these names as they say them.

WHAT TO WATCH FOR: Children who clap each syllable accurately. Children who are unsure, hesitant or imitate others. Children whose claps don't match the syllables

WHAT IF THE CHILD CANNOT COMPLETE THE TASK? Children who are unsure or inaccurate may benefit from the early awareness and syllable awareness activities in the following chapter. These are designed to help children become aware of the sound structure of words and divide them into syllables.

Clapping Words That Carry Meaning

WHAT WE WANT TO KNOW: Can the child clap each word she hears in a simple sentence when all the words carry meaning?

WHY WE WANT TO KNOW: A child must understand the concept of "word" in order to respond appropriately to reading instruction. It is easier to clap words — nouns and verbs — whose content carries meaning.

WHAT TO DO: To a small group, say, "I'm going to say a sentence. You say it again after me and clap your hands once for each word you hear." Model and practice with the children using one or two sentences such as, "Susan ran home," or "I ate pizza." Then invite them to do the same thing with three more sentences, such as, "My head hurts," "I see dad," and "Mike made cookies."

WHAT TO WATCH FOR: Children who clap for each word. Children who imitate others and are unsure about when to clap. Children who clap, but don't match the words. Children who match their claps to syllables rather than words.

WHAT IF THE CHILD CANNOT COMPLETE THE TASK? Children who are unsure or inaccurate may benefit from the word awareness activities in the following chapter. These help them practice matching spoken words to a discrete physical response and to printed words. Specialized techniques are provided for children who find this critical task confusing and difficult.

Clapping Words Including Function Words

WHAT WE WANT TO KNOW: Can the child clap each word he hears when some of the words are function words such as articles, prepositions and conjunctions?

WHY WE WANT TO KNOW: Children need to be able to recognize that function words such as "the," "a," "and," "to" and "for" are separate from the content words they are often closely connected to (e.g., "the ball," "a boy," "to school" and "for you"). The ability to precisely match spoken words to words in print is essential to reading.

WHAT TO DO: To a small group of children, say, "I'm going to say a sentence. You say it again after me and clap your hands once for each word you hear." Model and practice with sentences such as, "The dog ran to Nancy" and "She bought it for Tom." Then ask the children to clap three other sentences, such as, "I drove to the store," "She is sick today," and "Go to the back of the room."

WHAT TO WATCH FOR: Children who clap for each spoken word. Children who are unsure of when to clap or who imitate others. Children who clap but do not match each word.

WHAT IF THE CHILD CANNOT COMPLETE THE TASK? Children who are unsure or inaccurate may benefit from the word awareness activities in the following chapter.

Matching Spoken Words to Printed Words

WHAT WE WANT TO KNOW: Can the child point to each printed word in a familiar sentence as it is spoken?

WHY WE WANT TO KNOW: Recognizing the one-to-one correspondence between a spoken word and a printed word is a necessary prerequisite of learning to read. Until children can locate the word they are saying in the line of print, they will remain non-readers.

WHAT TO DO: Using a simple and familiar big book or dictated story — one that has been read before — ask each child to take a turn reading it aloud. Instruct them to point to each word as they say it. A pointer may be useful.

WHAT TO WATCH FOR: Children who point exactly to each word as it is said. Children who point to some words as they are said. Children who do not point to any words as they are said.

WHAT IF THE CHILD CANNOT COMPLETE THE TASK? Children who are not precise in matching spoken words to printed words may benefit from the word awareness activities in the following chapter. Specialized techniques are provided for children who find this task confusing or difficult.

Identifying Rhyming Words and Rhyming Parts of Words

WHAT WE WANT TO KNOW: Can the child identify words that rhyme? Can the child recognize the parts of rhyming words that are alike and the parts that are different?

WHY WE WANT TO KNOW: Recognizing the parts of rhyming words that are alike and the parts that are different indicates an awareness of phonemic segmentation, the concept of onset and rime, and the ability to use familiar words and parts of words to help decode unknown words.

WHAT TO DO: Use magnetic letters and a magnetic surface such as a cookie sheet, the side of a filing cabinet, or a magnetic chalkboard. Post three words, two of which rhyme, such as "cat," "fat" and "like." Point to and read aloud the words. Ask the children which two words rhyme. Model and practice the task. Post other sets of three words, asking which words rhyme.

Using one set of two rhyming words, ask the children which parts of these words sound the same. Ask each child to respond and show you the letters that are the same. Ask the children to show you the letters that are different. Repeat the task with other sets of rhyming words until you have observed each child's ability to complete the task.

WHAT TO WATCH FOR: Children who can identify the rhyming words. Children who can tell or show you the letters that are the same and the letters that are different. Children who can indicate the rhyming words but can't identify the letters that are the same and those that are different. Children who cannot identify the rhyming words.

WHAT IF THE CHILD CANNOT COMPLETE THE TASK? Children who cannot identify rhyming words and cannot locate the parts that are the same and different may benefit from the analogy awareness activities and all the reading activities in the following chapter.

Dividing Words into Phonemes

WHAT WE WANT TO KNOW: Can the child segment one-syllable words into discrete phonemes?

WHY WE WANT TO KNOW: In order to learn to read, children must be aware that words are composed of discrete sounds. Instruction in phonics will not be effective until this awareness is in place.

WHAT TO DO: Invite the child or children to create a story of one or two sentences about a story they have heard or read or a news event. Say the first word of the story to them. Ask them to repeat it slowly and think about what they hear at the beginning of the word. Ask individual children to come up and write on a chart or the chalkboard the letter they hear at the beginning of that word, the next letter, etc. Continue with each word of the story, giving every child an opportunity to contribute.

WHAT TO WATCH FOR: Children who can say the words slowly, hear the sounds and record some of them. Children who can say the words slowly and identify the letter sound, but can't write it. Children who can say the words slowly, but can't identify the letter sound. Children who can't say the word slowly, identify the sound, or write the letter.

WHAT IF THE CHILD CANNOT COMPLETE THE TASK? Children who cannot say the words slowly, identify the sounds or letters, or write the sounds or letters may benefit from the phoneme awareness activities in the following chapter.

PHONOLOGICAL AWARENESS OBSERVATION
INDIVIDUAL CHECKLIST

Student _____

Date _____

1. *Clapping Syllables*
   1. Accurate ☐
   2. Unsure ☐
   3. Unable ☐

2. *Clapping Words That Carry Meaning*
   1. Accurate ☐
   2. Unsure ☐
   3. Unable ☐

3. *Clapping Words Including Function Words*
   1. Accurate ☐
   2. Unsure ☐
   3. Unable ☐

4. *Matching Spoken Words to Printed Words*
   1. Accurate ☐
   2. Unsure ☐
   3. Unable ☐

5. *Identifying Rhyming Words and Rhyming Parts of Words*
   1. Accurate ☐
   2. Unsure ☐
   3. Unable ☐

6. *Dividing Words into Phonemes*

   Says word slowly, identifies letter and sound
   1. Accurate ☐
   2. Unsure ☐
   3. Unable ☐

   Identifies and writes letter and sound
   1. Accurate ☐
   2. Unsure ☐
   3. Unable ☐

PHONOLOGICAL AWARENESS OBSERVATION
CLASS RECORD

Date _____

Name	Syllables	Meaning Words	Non-Meaning Words	Matching	Rhyming	Phonemes

. . . .

INSTRUCTIONAL ACTIVITIES

The activities outlined in this chapter are designed to be integrated into a language arts program that emphasizes meaning-getting and meaning-giving in authentic reading and writing situations. Although phonological awareness is just one component of the complex process of learning to read and write, it is, nevertheless, critical and is highlighted in this book because its importance has not always been recognized. With this in mind, we hope that committed whole language teachers will support young readers in developing their phonological awareness.

The activities are organized developmentally starting with the earliest awareness of sound segmentation and continuing through to the most sophisticated stage, which involves consciously analyzing phonemic units. As children progress along this developmental continuum, their ability to set aside the message of the language to think about and analyze the language itself increases. This metalinguistic skill is both facilitated and necessitated by encounters with print.

The content and methodology of the activities in this chapter are based on research that suggests that phonological awareness is fostered when:

— Instructional activities are carefully planned.
— A portion of the activity time is spent on explicit direct instruction.
— Phonemic awareness is not presented as an isolated skill to be learned through drill, but is integrated into a meaning-based curriculum. In *Reading Recovery: A*

Guidebook for Teachers in Training, Marie Clay wrote, "Phonic awareness activities will not be helpful unless they can be placed in a context of real reading and writing. This can be accomplished by relating sound segmentation tasks to the actual things a child does when trying to read or spell a word. The value of being able to hear sounds in words can be emphasized by showing children how it helps them cross-check what they read with the letters they would expect to see in the printed word."

— Explicit and systematic activities are provided for students who are at risk, using activities and materials appropriate to their individual needs, interests and abilities.

Organization of the Activities

The activities are grouped into five developmental areas. All the activities are linked to sections of the previous chapter titled "Assessing Phonological Awareness." Using the information gleaned from an assessment of their level of phonological awareness is particularly important for children who are at risk. Though the instructional activities are designed for use with five- to seven-year-olds, they may also be appropriate for older students who need remedial instruction.

— Early awareness activities: Draw children's attention away from the meaning of words to the sound structure of the words.
— Syllable awareness activities: Help children begin to analyze the structure of words.
— Word awareness (sentence segmentation) activities: Help children recognize the one-to-one correspondence between spoken and printed words.
— Phoneme awareness activities: Help children develop decoding strategies based on the understanding that words comprise individual sounds.
— Analogy awareness activities: Help children read new words by recognizing and comparing similar sound clusters and spelling patterns in words.

Within each area, instructional activities are grouped into three categories:

— Integrated activities: Begin with suggestions for teaching the skills through direct instruction, and conclude with reading and writing activities that demonstrate ways of integrating the skills across the language arts curriculum.

Researchers encourage teachers to use literature to create a language-rich environment that helps turn children's attention to language itself. In a 1992 article in *The Reading Teacher*, Priscilla Griffith and Mary Olson wrote, "Probably the most accessible, practical, and useful vehicles to enhance students' sensitivity to the phonological basis of their language are children's books that deal playfully with speech sounds." Most of the suggestions for the reading and writing activities are based on specific children's books. The books recommended, however, are intended as examples only. The same techniques can be applied to a wide variety of children's literature.

Hallie Kay Yopp's 1995 article, "Read-Aloud Books for Developing Phonemic Awareness: An Annotated Bibliography," which appeared in the *Reading Teacher*, is an excellent resource that suggests alphabet books, rhyming books and books that deal playfully with the sound structure of words.

— Transition, management and center activities: Include miscellaneous ideas, tips, suggestions and strategies that not only increase phonological awareness, but also provide quick, meaningful activities that can be used during transition periods or down times, such as while students are waiting in line. Some of these can also be used as management techniques or ideas for literacy centers.

— Activities for children at risk: Designed specifically for children who need more support to develop their phonological awareness. The tasks are more individualized, structured and extended than the brief instructional detours intended for use in whole language classrooms.

Early Awareness Activities

When children learn to speak a language, they naturally become well-acquainted with its elementary speech sounds or phonemes. They pronounce these sounds with every word they say, and hear them in every utterance. Despite their remarkable expertise in using the sounds, however, children ordinarily spend little time thinking consciously about what they are doing. Their focus is quite properly on getting meaning and producing understandable messages. A conscious awareness of phonemes, however, is necessary as it has been shown that this understanding is strongly related to success in reading.

The early awareness activities outlined in this section help children begin to develop phonemic awareness by teaching them to analyze the sounds within words independent of the meaning of the words. They start with activities designed to help direct children's attention to non-verbal sounds, such as music, tapping, animal noises and other sounds commonly heard in the environment. Later, the focus changes to verbal sounds, which include rhyme and alliteration.

Direct Instruction

NON-VERBAL SOUNDS

Help students learn to pick out individual sounds in the context of other sounds by quietly assigning animal sounds to several students. Ask one student to make his noise first, then invite two or three others to join in so that there is a cacophony of sounds. As they do so, ask the other children to close their eyes, listen carefully and try to identify the individual sounds.

Play a drum and instruct students to march to its beat. Clap and march to the beat.

VERBAL SOUNDS

Alliteration

Alliteration occurs when two or more words in close conjunction begin with the same letter or sound. Many games, songs and poems can be used to expose children to alliteration. An enjoyable way to begin is to use their names or the names of common objects. Say a child's name, then add an alliterative sound after it (e.g., Meghan-Mo, Becky-Ba, Jeffrey-Ji). When children's names start with a vowel, simply omit the consonant sound (e.g., Anna-O, Anna-A, Anna-I).

Sing alliterative songs, such as "My Bonnie Lies over the Ocean." Invite the children to sit down or stand up every time they come to a word that starts with /b/. The last four lines of the song go very fast!

My Bonnie lies over the ocean.
My Bonnie lies over the sea.
My Bonnie lies over the ocean.
Oh, bring back my Bonnie to me, to me.
Bring back, bring back,
Oh bring back my Bonnie to me, to me.
Bring back, bring back,
Oh bring back my Bonnie to me.

Sing and act out an alliterative version of the classic "Teddy Bear." Discuss how many of the words begin with /t/.

Teddy Bear, Teddy Bear,
Turn around.
Teddy Bear, Teddy Bear,
Touch the ground.
Teddy Bear, Teddy Bear,
Tie your shoe.
Teddy Bear, Teddy Bear,
That will do.

Tell the children to imagine that they are going to be stranded on a desert island and can bring only one thing with them. The thing they choose must start with the same sound as their first name. Start things off by showing them what to say (e.g., I am Jasmine and I'm going to bring jewels). Then go around the group, asking the children to make similar statements using their own names.

Rhyme

Show your class what rhyme is by demonstrating some rhyming words. Every time you say a pair of rhyming words, make an obvious visual or auditory sign. For example, clap twice and say, "Mark." Clap twice more and say, "Dark."

Once the children have the idea, ask them to clap while you say the words, or ask a child to say one word while you add a rhyming word. Or ask one child to say a word and clap, then ask a second child to add a rhyming word and clap.

Say two rhyming words and ask the children to add a third.

Say a word and then throw a ball to a child. She is to say a word that rhymes with yours, then throw the ball to another child. It's often fun to include nonsense words in this activity. If a child can't think of a rhyming word, ask other students who know one to raise their hands and volunteer to have the ball thrown to them.

Hold up an object, say its name, and ask students to say words that rhyme with it.

When singing or reciting poetry, ask the children which words rhyme. Talk about which parts of the rhyming words sound similar and which parts sound different. You can even point out how the rhyming parts are spelled similarly.

Picture-sorting games are fun for children and can be set up at learning centers. Extend a favorite rhyming book by selecting rhyming words that can be portrayed in pictures. Glue the pictures to cards, and include pictures of some things that don't rhyme. Invite a child to sort the pictures into two piles: those that rhyme and those that don't. Beginning with three picture cards (two that rhyme and one that doesn't) makes it easy to master this task. Gradually increase the number of pictures.

Reading and Writing

READING

Choose books that make use of playful, rhyming and alliterative language. Even the most basic alphabet books often display sound-play qualities that help enhance phoneme awareness.

Maximize the impact of books that focus on the sound structure of language by being enthusiastic about the reading and directing the children with appropriate comments and questions. One way of doing this is to begin by reading the story or poem all the way through, just for fun. If it's appropriate, pause once or twice during the reading, inviting the students to insert a predictable word. During subsequent readings, comment on the way words rhyme or start with the same sound. Ask students to point out which parts of rhyming words sound the same and to predict what comes next. Ask them why they think the author chose certain words and why others would not fit.

Alphabears: An ABC Book by Kathleen Hague, illustrated by Michael Hague (Henry Holt, 1984). This simple book includes a great deal of alliteration and rhyme:

— Begin by reading and discussing *Alphabears*, using the suggested techniques.
— Invite the children to write or dictate a sentence using their own name. The sentence should be structured like one of the following:

M is for *Maddy*, who likes a *mulberry*.
M is for Maddy, who is *merry* all year.

When they have finished, ask them to illustrate what they have written or dictated. Compile the children's work into a class book and read it aloud.
— Invite the class to collaborate to think of another line that rhymes with each child's sentence. Here are some examples:

M is for Maddy who likes a mulberry.
She likes to eat it with a big cherry.

M is for Maddy who is merry all year.
Her favorite place is always right here.

Other books that help promote early phonemic awareness include:

— *Four Fur Feet* by Margaret Wise Brown (Doubleday, 1993). A great book for children who are just beginning to identify and attend to the sounds in words, this is the simple story of a furry animal who walks around the world. The phrase "four fur feet" is repeated in every sentence, drawing readers' attention to the /f/ sound.
— *I Can Fly* by Ruth Krauss (Golden Press, 1985). This book presents rhymes based on a child's imitation of the sounds of various animals. For example, the child squirms like a worm and observes, "A cow can moo, and I can too."

WRITING

Journal Writing
Make sure children have an opportunity to write in their own journals every day. Doing so encourages them to use invented spellings as they write and draw about both topics of their own choice and assigned topics. To focus on early phonological awareness skills, ask the children to write about things that rhyme or words that start with the same sound. They can include their part of the class book in their journal.

Many of the activities at this stage involve using the children's names. Even when they are just starting school, most children can read and write their own names. As a result, these words are familiar. And, because the children are constantly exposed to the names of other children, they tend to learn these too. The ability to read many names dramatically increases the number of words and letters they know, and provides a source of letters and words that can be used effectively in their reading and writing.

READ MY LIPS

Silently mouthing a child's name draws her attention to the way sounds are produced by the articulators — the mouth, tongue, teeth and lips — and encourages children to notice the changes that signal a new sound. This is a powerful tool in helping them discover that sounds are segmented.

A variety of games can spring from this activity. For example, invite the children to watch for you to mouth a name — signaling that a particular child is excused from an activity or that it is his turn to do something. When children become proficient at recognizing their own names, ask them to watch for and identify the names of others. When they tire of first names, use their last names. Children like games like this — and they produce a very quiet classroom!

FIND A NAME THAT STARTS LIKE YOURS

This game, which works best if it's introduced first to a small group, also stimulates listening to and looking for initial letters and sounds. Write the children's names on cards that can be placed on a pocket chart or a list that everyone can see easily.

Choose one child at a time to be the focus and invite everyone to read that child's name. Then read aloud the list of names together, looking and listening for a name that starts like the name of the chosen child. When the children hear or see one, they raise their hands. Help them check both the letter and sound to make sure they are right.

NAME AND VERB ALLITERATION

Use the names of children in the class to introduce and model this game. For example, you might say, "We are going to say

Jamal's name, then think of something that Jamal can do that starts with the same sound as his name. For example, we might say, 'Jamal jumps.' Let's work together to do the same thing with Michael's name: 'Michael m_____.'" Until they understand the game, you may need to help the children think of words. This game is useful while waiting in line or for getting the children's attention after they have made the transition to a new activity.

THINK OF A WORD

This game, which focuses attention on initial and final consonants, is a great device for bringing quiet to a group. Print the children's names on large cards. Hold up one of the cards and ask the children to think of a word that starts like the name on it. As they become more proficient, ask them to think of a word that ends like the name on the card. As the game becomes part of your classroom routine, the children will automatically think of a word that starts or ends like the name when you hold up a card.

A multi-sensory approach is often helpful with children who are having trouble identifying and segmenting sounds or words. Show a child how to feel the sounds that you ask him to hear or say. For example, you might model the following sequence with a child named Mark:

Teacher: Mark starts with the letter M and it sounds like /m/. You say /m/ and feel, like this, the side of your nose where that sound is made. It sort of vibrates, doesn't it? Now, let's look in the mirror and see what your mouth does when you say *m-m-m* for Mark. Yes, your lips are pressed together. Let's say Mark together. Do you see and hear /m/ at the beginning of Mark? Now let's say Mary. Mary starts like Mark. Let's feel the side of our noses to see if the same thing happens. Let's look in the mirror to see if it looks the same."

This kind of brief activity can be carried out with an individual or small group while the rest of the class is busy with other things. Parents can be encouraged to do the activity at home with their child, and a classroom assistant or volunteer could repeat the activity several times over a few days until the child understands the concept.

The phoneme-segmenting activity using Elkonin boxes, described in the phoneme awareness activities section of this chapter, is also helpful for children who are at risk.

Syllable Awareness Activities

The activities in this section are intermediate phonological awareness activities that require children not only to hear the sounds in language but also to analyze language and investigate the sounds that make up words. One of the ways of breaking a word into its constituent sounds is to divide it into syllables. Although this is not difficult for most young children, it is worth spending some time on, as it is a phonological awareness skill that they must possess in order to be able to learn to read.

Direct Instruction

COMPOUND WORDS

Because there is meaning attached to the separate words in compound words, distinguishing compound words is easiest for children and makes a good starting point for teaching them how to identify syllables.

Display pictures of a few things that are represented by compound words (e.g., sunset, sailboat, snowman). Point to one of the pictures and ask the children to name it and identify the two smaller words that make up its name. Ask them to say the words separately, then together. Now print a few compound words for the children to see. Print them first in one color, then again with the base word in a different color. Tell the children that you are going to study each word by paying attention to its parts. Explain that some words can be divided this way and some can't, and that you will start with words that can.

Write each word on a card and cut between the components. Hold a word together and say, for example, "This word is 'sunset.'" Then separate the parts and point out that one word is "sun" and the other is "set." Now put the words together and explain that when you put "sun" and "set" together, they make one word — "sunset." Do this with each word.

Brainstorm with the group to come up with a list of compound words. Invite the children to choose and illustrate one of the words. Compile their illustrations into a book.

IDENTIFYING SYLLABLES

Tell the children that another way to study words is to think about their stops. Explain that a stop or syllable is marked every time we hear ourselves stop when saying a word.

Start by clapping syllables, first saying aloud the children's own names, then other multi-syllabic words in their environment. Be sure to clap individual words rather than words in a sentence.

To add variety to this activity, bounce a ball, tap your finger, or spin around to correspond with the number of syllables in a word. You can also dance, march and walk in time with the syllabic intonation patterns of songs, words and poems.

As children grasp this concept, start writing the words, using a variety of techniques to represent the syllables. For example, you might begin by writing a child's name on the chalkboard, underlining each syllable. Then write each syllable in a different color, then place a magnetic marker above each.

At this stage, avoid focusing on the number of syllables in words — don't ask how many syllables are in a word or expect the children to think of a word with a given number of syllables. This may distract them from hearing the syllable divisions and thinking about the word itself.

SYNTHESIZING SYLLABLES

The object of this activity is to say a word slowly and encourage children to figure out what it is. This can be great fun if you use a puppet with a peculiar way of speaking who wants to give the children various presents. When he tells them what to expect, he can articulate the words slowly, syllable by syllable. The children enjoy figuring out what the puppet wants to give them.

Vary this game by using the children's names. For example, you might say, "I want someone to bring me a pencil. I want Jer— to bring me a pencil." If the class includes more than one child whose name starts with a particular sound, continue to the next syllable until the identity of the child you have chosen becomes clear.

Reading and Writing

READING

One Wide River to Cross, adapted by Barbara Emberley, illustrated by Ed Emberley (Little, Brown, 1966, 1992). The characters who star in this book are animals with short and long names, making it easy to compare word length.

— Read the book aloud as suggested in the early awareness activities section of this chapter. Be sure to develop a steady rhythm. The music provided in the back of the book may be helpful.
— Focus on the names of the animals that went into the ark. Animals are fun because many of them have very long

names. Comment on the length of an animal's name by saying things like, "Wow, hippopotamus is a long word. Listen to all the stops in it," and "Yak is a little word that has only one stop."

— Read aloud the entire story verse by verse. On a second reading, introduce an activity similar to the song "Bingo." Read aloud the sections that tell how many of each animal embarked on the ark. Then read these sections again, this time inviting the children to join you in clapping the syllables of each animal's name rather than saying it.

"The animals came in two by two
The alligator lost his shoe."

"The animals came in two by two
The (clap clap clap clap) lost his shoe."

— Write each animal's name on a large card and cut up the cards at the syllabic breaks. Mix up the pieces and pass them out to the students, one word at a time. Invite the children to put the words back together again, saying something like, "The first word we are going to put together is 'alligator.' Because there are four stops in it, four of you have letter cards. What is the first sound? Who has the letters that say /æl/?" Follow this procedure for each syllable of each word.

Other books that can be used to enhance syllable awareness include:

— *Eating the Alphabet: Fruits and Vegetables from A to Z* by Lois Ehlert (Harcourt Brace Jovanovich, 1989). This book lists all sorts of fruits and vegetables for each letter of the alphabet. The length of the words varies from one syllable (e.g., lime) to four (e.g., watermelon).
— *Sing a Song of Popcorn* by Beatrice Schenk de Regniers, Eva Moore, Jan Carr & Mary Michaels White (Scholastic, 1988). This is a book of poems that are especially good for teaching syllable segmentation because the rhythm makes the syllabic breaks more obvious.

Marking Syllables in Journals

Ask the children to mark the syllables of words as they write in their journals. They can do this by making a mark above or underlining each syllable. If you or the children would rather not make permanent marks in the journals, they can make temporary marks with plastic markers or cover the writing with a transparency and mark on that.

THE SAME NAMES

Print the children's names on strips of card or a large piece of paper, read them, and clap the syllables of each name. Choose one child's name at a time and clap its syllables with the children. For example, you might say, "Everyone clap the parts (or syllables) of José's name. If your name has the same number of syllables as José's, raise your hand. Let's clap your name to see if you're right." Repeat this process as many times as you wish.

As the children become familiar with this game, extend it to other situations, such as deciding which children line up first, second, etc. Say, "Everyone whose name has the same number of parts (or syllables) as Kevin's may line up first. Everyone whose name has the same number of syllables as Tamara's may line up next. The rest may line up after that." As the children take their places in line, encourage them to clap their names to make sure they are correct.

HOW MANY SYLLABLES ARE IN YOUR NAME?

Say, "Raise your hand if there are four (one, two, five, etc.) parts (syllables) in your name. Are you right? Everyone clap (child's) name to see if there are four syllables." This game can be used while waiting in line or as an attention-getting and quieting technique after the children have made the transition from one activity to another.

NAME SORT

This game works well as a literacy center activity. Print all the children's names on cards and place these in a container. Place one name of one syllable, one name of two syllables, and so on in another container to use as category headings for sorting the names in the first container. Show the children how to line up the heading names across a table, then sort the names of the other children into categories according to the number of syllables in each name.

Exaggerating the syllables when presenting names for syllable clapping can be helpful. Make each syllable clear and distinguishable (e.g., Da-*rush*, *Cait*-lin).

Movement and other sensory activities provide additional pathways to learning this skill. In addition to clapping, try banging a drum, cymbals or wooden blocks to mark the syllables in names.

Print familiar names on tag strips and cut them into syllables. Then choose one of the names and put the parts together, pronouncing each syllable as you do so. Than clap for each syllable. Model this process several times and repeat it using other names. Continue until the child can clap the syllables of familiar names without the visual example.

Word Awareness (Sentence Segmentation) Activities

Before they can learn to read proficiently, children must be able to recognize the one-to-one correspondence between words that are spoken and words that are written. In her book, *Becoming Literate*, Marie Clay wrote, "As long as the child cannot locate the word he is saying in the line of print, he will remain a non-reader."

Participating in simple pointing and clapping activities while learning to read helps children understand that there is a space between both written and spoken words that "the eye sees, the voice says, and the finger points." Learning this skill is difficult for some children. Do not expect to see it in their writing immediately.

The goal of the activities in this section is to help children hear and see the words within sentences as separate entities. This section follows the syllable awareness activities because research shows that matching a spoken word to a printed word in a sentence is more difficult for children than distinguishing syllables in spoken words.

Direct Instruction

MARKING WORDS WITH NOISE

Use noisemakers, such as a bouncing ball, ringing bell or clapping hands, to create a noise for each word of a spoken sentence. Begin by slowly saying a sentence that contains only familiar words that can be portrayed with pictures; that is, words that carry meaning (e.g., Jeff eats cookies). At this stage, avoid sentences that include function words, such as articles, prepositions and verbs like "is," that can't be portrayed with pictures.

Ask the class to repeat the entire sentence. Then repeat the sentence yourself, bouncing a ball as you say each word. Using a different noisemaker every time, ask the class to repeat each sentence two or three times with you. Because you must talk more slowly while bouncing a ball, using the ball as the first noisemaker before moving on to others is a good idea. When the children are ready, move on to include sentences containing words that can't be portrayed with pictures (e.g., Sherice is a girl).

MARKING AND POINTING TO WORDS

As you read aloud a poem or text to the children, use a pointer to mark each word. Ask the children to to do the same thing as you or they read a text.

Invite the children to dictate sentences. Write the sentences on sentence strips, cut them up, and put them back together with the children's help. Ask the children to leave spaces between the words.

Invite the children to work with a partner to take turns saying sentences and making corresponding noises.

Ask the children to count the number of words in a given sentence.

During oral reading, ask a child to read with her finger. Expect her to point exactly under the word she is saying.

Reading and Writing

Short, simple rhyming poems make excellent vehicles for teaching word awareness. Talk about how the words rhyme and place a mark above the rhyming words.

Write a short, rhyming poem on sentence strips, using a different color to print the last word of each line. Cut between the words. Read the poem together, pointing to each word as you read it. Scramble the words, read the scrambled version, and discuss whether the poem still makes sense. Pass out the last word of each line to several children. Read the poem together. When you reach the last word of each line, pause and have only the child holding the last word say it.

Down by the Bay by Raffi, illustrated by Nadine Bernard Westcott (Crown Publishers, 1987). The rhyme in this book, which is based on the familiar nonsense song, works particularly well as an aid for developing word awareness. The repeated chorus is easy to memorize and act out. Furthermore, the key words can easily be pictured in the children's heads, enabling them to isolate them from other words.

— Read the book, using the techniques suggested in the early awareness activities section of this chapter.
— On cards, print the 24-word chorus (Down by the bay / Where the watermelons grow / Back to my home / I dare not go ...). Line up 24 children and give each child, in order, one card. Ask the remaining children to walk down the line, pointing to each child and saying that child's word. If there aren't enough children remaining to do this, invite each child in the line to say his or her word. You can stand at the end of the line to say the verses "Mother" would say.

Another book that fosters word awareness is:

— *Dinosaur Chase* by Carolyn Otto (Harper Trophy, 1991). This book describes all sorts of things that dinosaurs do. The repetition of the word "dinosaur" enables children to see the word and separate it from the other words that describe what the dinosaur does.

Only when children grasp the concept that sentences are divided into words will they be able to apply this understanding to their writing. As their awareness of the "space between words" grows, it will begin to be reflected in their writing.

Journal Writing
When the children read their journals to you, ask them to point to each word as they read it. Ask them if they see a space on the page every time their voice makes a space. Instruct them to leave a space equal to the width of two fingers between words — and to check their work by placing two fingers between the words as they write them.

A small sticky note helps remind some children to leave spaces between words. As the child finishes writing a word, he places the sticky note at the end of the word. When he writes the next word, he picks up the note and places it after that word.

SHOW ME A LETTER — SHOW ME A WORD

Print a sentence or two on a piece of card. Read the sentence aloud, pointing to each word, then ask individual children to show you a letter or show you a word. Teach the children how to frame a word or letter with two fingers, so that when you ask them to do this in a structured activity or during reading or writing, they know exactly how to respond. Framing is a more exact and focused way of indicating a word or letter than pointing. Vary the sentences, using words of different lengths and different print sizes and styles, as well as different page layouts.

This activity can be carried out with a small group within the structure of a formal lesson or as a "password" activity for entering or leaving the classroom at recess or lunch. Children enjoy the password idea, and the activity flows smoothly and quickly if they know exactly how to respond and if you do it with only a few children each time.

MAKE A SENTENCE

Select a sentence — or several — from a familiar book. Print the sentence on a strip of card and cut it up into separate words. Place the cards in an envelope and print the page reference from the book on the outside. Store the book and envelope near a pocket chart or chalkboard tray. Show the children how to take out the words and arrange them in order on the tray or in the pockets. Though they should try to do as much as they can on their own, they can check the book if they need to. When finished, they can look in the book to confirm that they are correct.

This activity, which can be completed individually or with a partner, makes a good literacy center game.

A SPECIAL POINTER

When inviting children to point to and read material in big books or on experience charts and so on, use a variety of pointers, such as a flashlight, a magic wand, a light stick, long, stick-on plastic fingernails or other interesting or unusual objects. This adds interest and enhances the children's ability to match oral speech to printed words.

Set up an area where children can work in pairs to use an overhead projector to enlarge a familiar story printed on a transparency. The partners can take turns pointing to the words as they read the story from the screen or the transparency itself. Because children love to do this, it is a popular literacy center activity.

Arrange three objects in a row. Model pointing to each from left to right, but don't count the objects. Then ask the child to point to each object in left-to-right sequence. Increase the number of objects. Repeat the process, using objects such as shapes, colored disks, dots on paper, etc. As the child becomes more adept, ask her to say the name of each object as she points to it.

Invite a child to dictate a short sentence. Write the sentence on a strip and cut it up into words. Place the word cards in sequence on a table, leaving lots of space between the words. Model pointing to and reading the words, then ask the child to do the same. Repeat the process, gradually moving the words closer together.

When a child can do this task successfully, select a simple, one-line text and ask him to point and read. At first, some children may need a pointer to help them focus on each word.

When a child can read one line confidently, introduce texts containing two or three lines of print. Some children may require additional practice to return the finger and eyes to the beginning of a new line.

When children can point and read successfully, help them read more fluently by encouraging them to read with their eyes only.

Phoneme Awareness Activities

By analyzing words to identify the individual sounds and focusing on the sequence of sounds within words, the activities in this section help children understand that words comprise individual sounds. Extensive research indicates that phonemic awareness is an important prerequisite for understanding the alphabetic principle — that printed letters represent speech sounds.

Direct Instruction

INTERACTIVE WRITING

The ability to distinguish the sounds of oral language can be learned most easily if children use what they already know to help them learn what they need to know; in other words, children who use the sounds they produce in speech to learn the letters of the alphabet may be more successful at learning to read and write than those who try to learn the letters and then attach sounds to them.

Reading and writing are reciprocal processes, which means that learning in one mode helps foster learning in the other. Interactive writing, a technique developed for early literacy classrooms by Gay Su Pinnell and Andrea McCarrier, draws on this principle to help teach children to hear the sounds in words and record the letters that represent these sounds. It involves the children and teacher in working together to write stories, letters, recipes, lists, invitations, news, poems and anything else of interest or meaning to the class.

Interactive writing differs from shared writing, where the teacher uses the children's suggestions to model the writing process, in that the children themselves write as much of the text as they can, with the teacher providing only what they cannot.

With Five- and Six-Year-Olds

Interactive writing helps five- and six-year-olds who are just starting school hear and record sounds and learn the basic conventions of writing as they compose text. Very early in the year, the teacher gathers a group of children or the whole class around a paper chart pad and suggests that they write about something meaningful. This may be, for example, a story they have read, an event that took place, or a list of supplies they need for making modeling clay. During the initial sessions, the teacher shows the children how to say words slowly, isolate each sound, and draw on their knowledge of the spelling of their own names to record letters they know.

A typical early lesson might proceed like this:

Teacher: Today, we read a story about Dan, the flying man. We all liked the story. Who remembers what happened in the story? Yes, the people ran fast to catch Dan. Let's all say this:

"The people ran fast to catch Dan." The first word in our story is "the." I'll write "the." After "the" comes "people" — "the people." Let's say "people" slowly. Stretch it out. (Teacher models saying the word slowly, but not breaking up the sounds.) What sound do you hear at the beginning of the word "people"? Yes, I hear /p/ too. Patricia, you have a P at the beginning of your name. Come up here, please, and write the P for us.

The teacher continues to model the process by saying each word slowly, asking for responses, and encouraging the children to write letters from their own names that they already know. At first, the teacher provides most of the letters, but the children are expected to contribute more as the year progresses.

With Six- and Seven-Year-Olds
When used with six- and seven-year-olds, the technique continues to emphasize teaching the children to articulate words slowly, isolate sounds, and record letters they know. During a typical session, the children sit in front of the teacher, who is standing next to a blank chart paper pad. When the teacher calls on them, the children come up to write a word or parts of a word on the chart paper, leaving a hand's space between words. If they can't finish a word, the teacher calls on another child for help. If a child writes an incorrect letter, cover it with liquid paper or correction tape. Encourage the child to practice writing the correct letter on the chalkboard or in the air, then try again on the chart paper.

Here's how a session focusing on writing an invitation to parents to come to an open house might proceed:

The teacher begins by explaining that the class is going to write the invitation together and asks the children to suggest a way to start. The children decide to begin by saying, "Please come to our class open house."

Teacher: Our first word is "please." Everyone say "please." Who knows how to write the first part of "please"? Melanie, come up and write the /pl/, please. What's the next sound you hear in "please"? Did you hear what Cindy said? She said /i/. Cindy, please come up and write an E. I'll add an A. There is a silent A in "please." I'll write it here. What sound do we hear at the end of "please"? Yes, Daisy, I hear /z/, too. In this word, we use an S, just as in Daisy's name. Please come up and write the S. I'll add the silent E at the end. Everybody read this word. Next is the word "come." Everybody say "come." How are we going to write "come"?

The teacher continues to guide the children through the writing of the sentence, pausing after each word is added to say, "So far, what do we have? Everyone read with me."

When the sentence is finished, the teacher asks a volunteer to point to the words with a pointer as the class reads the sentence. This part of the process is repeated several times, with different children pointing to the words.

Because this process can take some time, plan to complete only about one sentence in each session.

With Older Children

Interactive writing can also be used with older children, though the emphasis shifts to more sophisticated skills like elaborating the story, punctuating correctly, and organizing paragraphs. Although the teacher continues to support the students by modeling and contributing as necessary, the children themselves do more and more of the writing.

Other Phoneme Awareness Activities

Ask the children to say a word that begins or ends with the same sound as another word, or has a similar sounding middle. Say, "Name a word that begins like 'cat' — /k/," "Name a word that ends like 'pen' — /p/" or "Name a word that has a middle like 'keen' — /i/."

Take a walk challenging the children to find items that begin with a selected sound.

Have fun combining adjectives and nouns that begin with the same sound (e.g., messy mommy, small snail, tiny Tim).

Reading and Writing

READING

Sing a Song of Popcorn by Beatrice Schenk de Regniers, Eva Moore, Jan Carr & Mary Michaels White (Scholastic, 1988). Many poems in this book playfully make use of phoneme substitution, deletion and addition. The following is a sample phoneme awareness activity using the poem "Weather," by Eve Merriam:

— Read the poem several times and discuss the fact that it is tricky because the words look almost the same, but one sound is different. Show the children what you mean by reading the line "Spack a spack speck flick a flack fleck." Write this line on the chalkboard or a sentence strip for the class to see. Read it several times, encouraging the children to read it with you. Say it again, substituting a different vowel sound (e.g., Spook a spook spook flook a flook flook) or vowel-sound pattern (e.g., Spack a spack speck flack a flack fleck). Ask the students to make up different words using these as a basis.

— Discuss how the words "puddle" and "jump" can be turned into "juddle" and "pump." Invite the children to help you to think of other pairs of words to mix up like this. The combinations can be endless.

Other books that play around with and manipulate phonemes include:

— *Fox in Socks* by Dr. Seuss (Beginning Books, 1965). In this book of tongue twisters, a mischievous fox, who wears socks, leads the ill-fated Mr. Knox through a series of funny situations. Though each section starts simply, the verbal complexity rapidly increases.

— *The Hungry Thing* by Jan Slepian & Ann Seidler (Follett Publishing, 1967). A friendly monster comes to town wearing a sign that says Feed Me. Though he asks for food, nobody can figure out what he wants because he mixes up the initial sounds of words (e.g., he asks for boop with a smacker, rather than soup with a cracker). Finally, a little boy sorts it out.

MOVABLE LETTERS

Using letters that can be moved around, such as magnetic letters or letter cards, provides a concrete representation that helps children understand that words are made up of individual letters as well as clusters or chunks of letters. Physically placing the letters in left-to-right sequence helps them grasp the sequence of letters in words. In addition, manipulating and substituting letters helps them understand onset and rime, as well as prefixes and grammatical endings (e.g., "-s," "-ed" and "-ing"), and helps them recognize spelling patterns.

Movable letters may be used for small-group or whole-class instruction or as a literacy center activity. Magnetic letters and a cookie sheet can be used to illustrate how words work during a guided reading or writing lesson.

OVERHEAD DEMO

Movable letters may be used on an overhead projector to show how letters and clusters of letters can be manipulated to change words, to model arranging letters in sequence, and to show the class how to check the accuracy of an arrangement of letters.

ELKONIN BOXES

Hearing Sounds in Words

Elkonin boxes — boxes divided into the number of sounds that make up a particular pictured word — are a useful tool for helping children distinguish the sounds in words. They can help teach children to attend specifically to the sounds in a word before they try to write the word and can also be used to teach the sequence of sounds in words. At this early stage, the focus is on sounds. No letters or printed words are used.

Collect pictures of familiar objects whose names are made up of three or four easily heard sounds. Below each picture, make a rectangle and divide it into squares representing the sounds — not the letters — in the name of the object. An example using the word "cat" is shown here.

The teacher begins by slowly saying "cat," emphasizing each sound, then asking the children to say the word slowly. It is important for them to slow down enough to hear the individual sounds, but not so much that the sounds are distorted or pronounced as choppy units. It is sometimes helpful to ask them to watch your lips as you say the word and feel their lips move as they say each sound.

The next phase involves modeling the activity, using counters or pennies to represent the sounds in the word. First, place a marker directly under each of the boxes. Say "cat" again very slowly. As you articulate each sound, push a counter into the corresponding box. Then encourage the children to do this themselves. If a child needs help, you can articulate the word while she moves the counters. Then switch roles, so that she articulates the word while you place the counters. The goal, however, is for the child to both say the word and move the counters herself.

Hearing and Recording the Sounds in Words
Start by completing an activity using Elkonin boxes as described in the previous sequence. Once the counters are in place, tell the children that you are going to write the word. Then ask, "What sounds do you hear?" When a child identifies a sound, ask him where it goes and tell him to write it in the correct box. Although the child may identify any of the sounds in any order, the letters must be entered in the correct box. If he needs help writing the letters, write them for him or provide movable plastic letters for him to use. To help him identify the letters, it may be necessary to ask questions such as, "What else can you hear?" "What do you hear at the beginning?" "What do you hear in the middle?" or "What do you hear at the end?"

Some children have a harder time with vowels than with consonants. In these cases, you may need to fill in the vowels while they record the consonants.

Moving On
Once children can successfully complete the activities described in the previous sections, they are ready to move on to more challenging tasks:

Complete the activity omitting the sequence using the counters.

Help the children fill in the boxes in sequence from left to right.

Give the children a picture with Elkonin boxes below it and ask them to fill in the boxes independently.

From time to time, use Elkonin boxes to help children who ask how to write words they want to include in individual writing activities. Do not do this every time, however. Use it only for words in which it is easy to hear the sounds, for frequently used words, and for words that are spelled the way they sound, such as "dark" and "park."

Analogy Awareness Activities

Analogy awareness involves recognizing and using familiar words or letter clusters to help read or write unfamiliar words. Usha Goswami and Felicity Mead found that this was a useful strategy for helping children as young as five read and write new words. In fact, soon after they begin to read and write, children can use their familiarity with certain letter clusters to decode new words. They may, for example, look for similarities in onsets and rimes. Research shows that teaching children to read new words by drawing on their knowledge of similar onsets and rimes is as effective as teaching them to draw on their knowledge of phonemes. If they can use both strategies, they have a larger repertoire of decoding techniques to draw on.

It's worth noting that English pronunciation and spelling patterns are loaded with inconsistencies (e.g., "some" and "home," "do" and "go"). When children happen upon these, simply explain that not all words fit into predictable patterns: some are just different.

Movable letters, chalkboards and whiteboards are excellent aids when children are completing analogy awareness activities because they make it easy to manipulate letters.

Direct Instruction

ANALYZING ANALOGIES

Write a word like "ring" on the chalkboard and suggest that the children imagine that they are detectives who must figure out how to read this word. Then write the word "sing" — or a similar rhyming word they know — and read it aloud. Explain that because they know that this word says "sing," they can use clues from it to help them read the unknown word.

Begin by asking what letter combinations are the same in both words. Talk about the sound made by the letter cluster "ing" in "sing" and point out that this is probably the ending sound of the unknown word as well. Then, draw their attention to other words they know that start with R (e.g., "ride," "run" and "red"). Help them combine the /r/ sound from these words with the "ing" chunk from the word "sing" in order to read the word "ring." Using movable letters is a powerful way to help children learn this strategy.

Write simple, snappy sentences containing rhyming words such as:

Uncle Mike rides a bike.
Now where is my cow?
Why is that bug playing in your rug?

Read the sentence to the class, leaving out the last word of the rhyming pair. Suggest that the children use their detective skills to help figure out how to read the words you left out. Then ask them to check the word to see if it makes sense in the sentence.

Choose some common rimes (e.g., "-at," "-ig" and "-ight") and use them to make word families. An extensive list of common rimes is found in *The Reading Teacher's Book of Lists* by Edward B. Fry, Jacqueline Kress and Donna Fountoukidis. Work with the class to brainstorm words that can be added to the word families you are creating. If a child suggests a word that has an ending that sounds the same but is spelled differently, include it but note the different spelling. Record the words as the children suggest them and read the list together several times. Then compose a class story using as many of the words as possible.

Sorting activities help children discriminate sounds and discover letter patterns and rules of spelling. Their active involvement engages them more fully in these activities and promotes the internalizing of patterns and rules more powerfully than using workbooks and rote memorization.

A sequence of activities might begin with sorting picture cards according to their initial sounds. As the children become more proficient at this, they can move on to sorting word cards. At first, choose pictures that represent words that begin with frequently occurring consonants, such as B, M, R and S. When children can sort these successfully, move on to sorting words with similar initial consonant blends, then similar vowels and digraphs.

As children's reading vocabulary grows, they can begin to sort pictures and words they know into categories defined by their beginning sounds, ending sounds or middle sounds. For example, you might ask them to find pictures of words that have the same middle sound as "fish."

The materials for sorting activities can be stored in envelopes placed inside file folders.

USING MOVABLE LETTERS

Physically manipulating letters stimulates learning. Provide individual children with a selection of letters and suggest that they use them to make a word they know. Then instruct them to take the word apart and put it back together again. Ask them to say the word and move their finger under the letters as they say the sounds.

Choose a couple of words with similar rimes, such as "sat" and "cat." Using the letters, model making and reading each word. Then, give a child the letters that make up a different rhyming word, such as "bat," and ask her to make this word. Point out the similarities and differences in the three words. Ask her to take away the "at" chunk, then recreate the word by putting it back.

Give a child the letters needed to make a word such as "can," then give him an M and ask him to change "can" to "man."

Do the same with other rhyming pairs, such as "like" and "bike." Construct one of the words yourself. Give the child the letters necessary to make the other word and ask him to construct it.

Extend this activity by inviting the children to choose the words themselves. They may think of the initial word themselves, make a word that rhymes with a word you have chosen, or make two or three words that sound like each other.

Reading and Writing

READING

Who Is Tapping at My Window? by A.G. Deming, illustrated by Monica Wellington (Dutton Children's Books, 1994). This simple, predictable rhyming book contains many words with phonemes that can be easily manipulated. Many of the rhyming words are the names of animals:

cat — rat
wren — hen
fox — ox
loon — raccoon
cony — pony
dog — frog
bear — hare

— Write the rhyming pairs on the chalkboard or chart paper where the children can see them easily. Ask the children questions like: "What is it about 'cat' and 'rat' that sound the same?" "What sounds in the two words are different?" "What word do we make if we replace the /r/ sound in 'rat' with a /k/ sound?" and "What word do we make if we replace the /k/ sound in 'cat' with the /r/ sound?"
— Encourage the children to think about how the words change as phonemes are added or deleted by asking questions like: "How does 'cony' sound if you add a /l/ sound right after the /k/ sound?" "How does 'pony' sound if you add a /l/ sound right after the /p/ sound?" "What word do we make if we start both 'cony' and 'pony' with the /b/ sound?"

Not all children who can successfully break up words into sounds can use this skill to help them read. Some need additional guidance to help them transfer the skill. Show them how to check to make sure the word they think they're reading is correct. Say, for example, "Let's read the first word. What do you think it is?" When they respond, "Cat," say, "Are you sure? How do you know that? Does the word have all the letters you think 'cat' should have? Say (or write) 'cat.' What sound do you hear at the beginning? In the middle? At the end? Now check the word and see if it really is 'cat.' Does it have the letter for /k/ at the beginning, /æ/ in the middle, and /t/ at the end? Whenever you read a word, you can look at it again to see if it has all the parts that you think it should."

WRITING

Journal Writing
As the children write in their journals, ask them to note words that begin or end with the same sound as other words. Encourage them to use the techniques you have practiced together to help them write new words.

Help children make up one-line rhymes by starting a sentence and leaving one of the words blank (e.g., My cat wears a __). Ask them what kind of clothing rhymes with the word "cat." Invite them to help you write the word in the blank. Follow the detective process outlined previously to write the missing word.

Encourage the children to write stories on sentence strips and cut some of the words between the onset and rime.

COMMERCIAL GAMES

Some commercial games encourage children to find similarities in words. The object of games like Junior Boggle and Boggle, for example, is to make as many words as possible within a time limit. As they play, children discover that they can make many more words if they generate several words from a particular rime or word pattern. These games make excellent center or rainy-day activities, and can be recommended to parents for fun at home.

WORD WALLS

Many teachers display lists of words on their classroom walls. If the words are sorted according to spelling patterns, the children can refer to the word wall when reading and writing. As they write or read words that fit into a particular category (e.g., words that contain the "ew" ending), they can add these to the list. As they collect, sort, categorize and display these words, the children discover patterns and rules.

WORD-SORT CONCENTRATION

This is an excellent center activity or rainy-day game. Make a set of word cards that include two or three words from several word families (e.g., try, fly, sky; tree, see, bee; bring, sing, ring) and place them face down on a table. Instruct the children to take turns trying to turn up two or three cards from the same word family. They might also make up a set of cards they can use to play the game at home.

The on-the-spot teaching moments described here should be brief and clear. They may need to be repeated several times in order to establish the principle of using known parts or patterns to decode new words.

When working with a group of children who need special help, have handy a white board and marker, a cookie sheet and magnetic letters or other movable letters that can be manipulated on a flat surface. When a child is unable to read a word in a text, try several prompts or techniques to help her find a strategy for decoding it. Using movable letters to generate and sort words by physically manipulating onsets and rimes may help children see patterns in words and apply these patterns when decoding other words.

Place two or three word cards (e.g., "ran," "sat," and "go") on a table. Provide enough movable letters for the children to add two rhyming words under each card. Once a child has done this, ask him to remove the part of each word in the family that is the same. Then ask him to recreate the word by replacing the chunk he removed. Ask him to remove the part of each word that is different, then replace these chunks.

If you know that the child can recognize a word that has the same rime as a word that is presenting a problem, show her how to use this knowledge to decode the unknown word. Suppose, for example, that a child is having trouble reading the word "mad," but you know that she can read "dad." You might say, "You know the word 'dad.' Let's write it together." Write "dad" with movable letters or on the whiteboard, then add, "If you know 'dad,' you can read this word." Write "mad." The child will probably be able to say "mad," giving her a powerful example of how to use what she already knows to decode a new word.

As an alternative, guide the child to make the link between a known and an unknown word by asking, "Do you know a word that ends like that?"

Model for the child how to isolate a chunk of the unknown word that he knows by saying, "Can you find a part (or chunk) in that word that you know?" Show him how to frame the part he knows. This may provide enough support for him to use what he already knows to figure out how to read the part he doesn't know.

Children who are having trouble using movable letters to represent the sounds they hear may need more practice with Elkonin boxes (see p. 78).

. . . .

REFERENCES AND RESOURCES

Adams, M.J. *Beginning to Read: Thinking and Learning about Print.* Cambridge, Mass: MIT Press, 1990.

Adams, M.J. "Why Not Phonics in Whole Language?" In *All Language and the Creation of Literacy* (W. Ellis, Ed.). Baltimore, Md: Orton Dyslexia Society, 1991.

Alegria, J., E. Pignot & J. Morais. "Phonetic Analysis of Speech and Memory Codes in Beginning Readers." In *Memory and Cognition.* Vol. 10: 1982.

Anderson, R.C., E.H. Hiebert, J.A. Scott & I.A.G. Wilkinson. *Becoming a Nation of Readers.* Champaign, Ill.: University of Illinois, Center for the Study of Reading, 1985.

Ball, E.W. "Assessing Phoneme Awareness." In *Language, Speech and Hearing Services in Schools.* Vol. 24: 1993.

Ball, E.W. & B.A. Blachman. "Phoneme Segmentation Training: Effect on Reading Readiness." In *Annals of Dyslexia.* Vol. 38: 1988.

Ball, E.W. & B.A. Blachman. "Does Phoneme Awareness Training in Kindergarten Make a Difference in Early Word Recognition and Developmental Spelling?" In *Reading Research Quarterly.* Vol. 26, no. 1: 1991.

Bear, D., M. Invernizzi, F. Johnston & S. Templeton. *Words Their Way.* Englewood Cliffs, N.J.: Prentice-Hall, 1996.

Blachman, B.A. "Early Literacy Acquisition: The Role of Phonological Awareness." In *Language and Learning Disabilities in*

School-Age Children and Adolescents (G. Wallach & K. Butler, Eds.). New York, N.Y.: Macmillan College Publishing, 1994.

Blachman, B.A., E. Ball, S. Block & D. Tangel. "Kindergarten Teachers Develop Phoneme Awareness in Low-Income, Inner-City Classrooms: Does It Make a Difference?" In *Reading and Writing: An Interdisciplinary Journal.* Vol. 6, no. 1: March 1994.

Bradley, L. & P. Bryant. "Categorizing Sounds and Learning to Read: A Causal Connection." In *Nature.* Vol. 30: 1983.

California Department of Education. *Every Child a Reader: The Report of the California Reading Task Force.* Sacramento, Calif.: California Department of Education, 1995.

Catts, H. "Phonological Processing Deficits and Reading Disabilities." In *Reading Disabilities: A Developmental Language Perspective.* (A. Kamki & H. Catts, Eds.). Boston, Mass: Allyn & Bacon, 1989.

Catts, H.W. "Keeping on Track to the Twenty-First Century." In *Learning Disabilities in School-Age Children and Adolescents.* (G. Wallach & K. Butler, Eds.). New York, N.Y.: Macmillan College Publishing, 1994.

Cazden, C. *Whole Language Plus.* New York, N.Y.: Teachers College Press, 1992.

Chall, J. *Learning to Read: The Great Debate.* New York, N.Y.: McGraw-Hill, 1967.

Clay, M. *Becoming Literate.* Portsmouth, N.H.: Heinemann, 1991.

Clay, M. *Reading Recovery: A Guidebook for Teachers in Training.* Portsmouth, N.H.: Heinemann, 1993.

Clay, M. *An Observation Survey.* Portsmouth, N.H.: Heinemann, 1993.

Cunningham, A.E. "Explicit Versus Implicit Instruction in Phonemic Awareness." In *Journal of Experimental Child Psychology.* Vol. 50: 1990.

Elkonin, D.B. "U.S.S.R." In *Comparative Reading* (J. Downing, Ed.). New York, N.Y.: Macmillan, 1973.

Flesch, R. *Why Johnny Can't Read.* New York, N.Y.: Harper & Row, 1955.

Fry, E.B., J.E. Kress & D.L. Fountoukidis. *The Reading Teacher's Book of Lists* (3rd ed.). Englewood Cliffs, N.J.: Prentice-Hall, 1993.

Goswami, U. & P. Bryant. *Phonological Skills and Learning to Read.* East Sussex, England: Lawrence Erlbaum Associates, 1990.

Goswami, U. & F. Mead. "Onset and Rime Awareness and Analogies in Reading." In *Reading Research Quarterly.* Vol. 27, no. 2: 1992.

Griffith, P.L. & M. Olson. "Phonemic Awareness Helps Beginning Readers Break the Code." In *The Reading Teacher.* Vol. 45, no. 7: 1992.

Haskell, D., B. Foorman & P. Swank. "Effects of the Orthographic/Phonological Units on First Grade Reading." In *Remedial and Special Education.* Vol. 13, no. 2: 1992.

Juel, C. "Phonemic Awareness: What Is It?" In *The Leadership Letters: Issues and Trends in Reading and Language Arts.* Parsippany, N.J.: Silver Burdett Ginn, 1996.

Juel, C. "The Role of Decoding in Learning to Read." In *American Educator.* Vol. 8: 1995.

Juel, C., P.L. Griffith & P.B. Gough. "Acquisition of Literacy: A Longitudinal Study of Children in First and Second Grade." In *Journal of Educational Psychology.* Vol. 78: 1986.

Juel, C. "Learning to Read and Write: A Longitudinal Study of 54 Children from First through Fourth Grades." In *Journal of Educational Psychology.* Vol. 80: 1988.

Kantrowitz, B. "The Reading Wars." In *Newsweek.* Fall-Winter, 1990.

Kirk, S. & W.D. Kirk. "How Johnny Learns to Read." In *Exceptional Children.* Vol. 22: 1956.

Lee, D. & L. Lamoreaux. *Learning to Read through Experience.* New York, N.Y.: Appleton-Century Crofts, 1943.

Liberman, I.Y., D. Shankweiler, F.W. Fischer & B. Carter. "Explicit Syllable and Phoneme Segmentation in the Young Child." In *Journal of Experimental Child Psychology.* Vol. 18: 1974.

Lundberg, I., J. Frost & O. Peterson. "Effects of An Extensive Program for Stimulating Phonological Awareness in Preschool Children." In *Reading Research Quarterly.* Vol. 23: 1988.

Mather, N. "Whole-Language Reading Instruction for Students with Learning Disabilities: Caught in the Cross Fire." In *Learning Disabilities and Practice*. Vol. 7: 1992.

Morais, J. "Constraints on the Development of Phonemic Awareness." In *Phonological Processes in Literacy: A Tribute to Isabelle Y. Liberman* (S.A. Brady & D.P. Shankweiler, Eds.). Hillsdale, N.J.: Erlbaum Associates, 1991.

O'Conner, R.E., A. Notori-Syverson & P.F. Vadasky. "Ladders to Literacy: The Effects of Teacher-Led Phonological Activities for Kindergarten Children with and without Disabilities." In *Exceptional Children*. Vol. 63, no. 1: 1996.

Oloffson, A. & I. Lundberg. "Can Phonemic Awareness Be Trained in Kindergarten?" In *Scandinavian Journal of Psychology*. Vol. 24: 1983.

Pearson, P.D. "Reclaiming the Center: An Apology for Seeking Common Ground in Teaching Reading." In *The First R* (D. Graves. M. Vandenbrock & B. Taylor, Eds.). New York, N.Y.: Teacher's College Press, Columbia University, 1996.

Pinnell, G.S. & A. McCarrier. "Interactive Writing: A Transition Tool for Assisting Children in Learning to Read and Write." In *Getting Reading Right from the Start: Effective Early Literacy Interventions* (E. Hiebert & B. Taylor, Eds.). Needham Heights, Mass.: Allyn & Bacon, 1994.

Routman, R. *Literacy at the Crossroads*. Portsmouth, N.H.: Heinemann, 1996.

Sawyer, D.J., C. Dougherty, M. Shelly & I. Spaanenburg. "Auditory Segmenting Performance and Reading Acquisition." In *Communication Skills and Classroom Success: Assessment of Language-Learning Disabled Students* (C.S. Simon, Ed.). Austin, Tex: Pro-Ed, 1991.

Share, D.L., A.F. Jorm, B. Maclean & R. Matthewes. "Sources of Individual Differences in Reading Achievement." In *Journal of Educational Psychology*. Vol. 76: 1984.

Stanovich, K.E. "Romance and Reality." In *The Reading Teacher*. Vol. 47, no. 4: 1993-1994.

Stanovich, K.E., A.E. Cunningham & B. Cramer. "Assessing Phonological Awareness in Kindergarten: Issues of Task Comparability." In *Journal of Experimental Child Psychology*. Vol. 38: 1984.

Stanovich, K.E., A.E. Cunningham & D.J. Freeman. "Intelligence, Cognitive Skills and Early Reading Progress." In *Reading Research Quarterly*. Vol. 19: 1984.

Stanovich, K.E. "Toward an Interactive-Compensatory Model of Individual Differences in the Development of Reading Fluency." In *Reading Research Quarterly*. Vol. 16: 1980.

Tangel, D. & B.A. Blachman. "Effect of Phoneme Awareness Instruction on Kindergarten Children's Invented Spelling." In *Journal of Reading Behavior*. Vol. 24, no. 2: 1992.

Uhry, J.K. & M.J. Shepherd. "Segmentation/Spelling Instruction as Part of a First-Grade Reading Program: Effects on Several Measures of Reading." In *Reading Research Quarterly*. Vol. 28: 1993.

Wallach, M.A. & L. Wallach. *Teaching All Children to Read*. Chicago, Ill.: University of Chicago Press, 1976.

Williams, J. "Teaching Decoding with an Emphasis on Phoneme Analysis and Phoneme Blending." In *Journal of Educational Psychology*. Vol. 72: 1980.

Wise, B.W., R.K. Olson & R. Treiman. "Subsyllabic Units as Aids in Beginning Readers' Word Learning: Onset-Rime versus Post-Vowel Segmentation." In *Journal of Experimental Child Psychology*. Vol. 49: 1990.

Yopp, H.K. "The Validity and Reliability of Phonemic Awareness Tests." In *Reading Research Quarterly*. Vol. 23: 1988.

Yopp, H.K. "Read-Aloud Books for Developing Phonemic Awareness: An Annotated Bibliography." In *The Reading Teacher*. Vol. 48, no. 6: 1995.

Yopp, H.K. "A Test for Assessing Phonemic Awareness in Young Children." In *The Reading Teacher*. Vol. 49, no. 1: 1995.

MORE TITLES FROM THE PIPPIN TEACHER'S LIBRARY

Helping Teachers Put Theory into Practice

STORYWORLDS
Linking Minds and Imaginations through Literature
MARLENE ASSELIN, NADINE PELLAND, JON SHAPIRO

Using literature to create rich opportunities for learning.

WRITING PORTFOLIOS
A Bridge from Teaching to Assessment
SANDRA MURPHY, MARY ANN SMITH

*How portfolios can help students become active partners
in the writing process.*

SUPPORTING STRUGGLING READERS
BARBARA J. WALKER

*Building on struggling readers' strengths to help them broaden
their strategies for making sense of text.*

ORAL LANGUAGE FOR TODAY'S CLASSROOM
CLAIRE STAAB

*Integrating speaking and listening into the curriculum to help
children discover the power of language.*

AN EXCHANGE OF GIFTS
A Storyteller's Handbook
MARION V. RALSTON

*Imaginative activities to enhance language programs
by promoting classroom storytelling.*

INFOTEXT
Reading and Learning
KAREN M. FEATHERS

*Classroom-tested techniques for helping students overcome
the reading problems presented by informational texts.*

WRITING IN THE MIDDLE YEARS
MARION CROWHURST

*Suggestions for organizing a writing workshop approach
in the classroom.*

IN ROLE
Teaching and Learning Dramatically
PATRICK VERRIOUR

A leading drama educator demonstrates how easily drama can be used to integrate learning across the curriculum.

LINKING MATHEMATICS AND LANGUAGE
Practical Classroom Activities
RICHARD MCCALLUM, ROBERT WHITLOW

Practical, holistic ideas for linking language—both reading and writing—and mathematics.

THE MONDAY MORNING GUIDE TO COMPREHENSION
LEE GUNDERSON

Strategies for encouraging students to interact with, rather than react to, the information they read.

LANGUAGE, LITERACY AND CHILDREN
WITH SPECIAL NEEDS
SALLY ROGOW

How primary teachers can support children with special needs, ensuring that they are able to truly participate in mainstream classrooms.

AN ENGLISH TEACHER'S SURVIVAL GUIDE
Reaching and Teaching Adolescents
JUDY S. RICHARDSON

The story of an education professor who returns to a high-school classroom determined to put theory into practice.

THOUGHTFUL TEACHERS, THOUGHTFUL LEARNERS
A Guide to Helping Adolescents Think Critically
NORMAN UNRAU

How teachers in all disciplines can use listening, talking, questioning, reading and writing to help students become thoughtful learners.

FUSING SCIENCE WITH LITERATURE
Strategies and Lessons for Classroom Success
CAROL M. KING, PEG SUDOL

Step-by-step lesson plans for integrating literature and science with nine- to 11-year-olds.

THE PIPPIN TEACHER'S LIBRARY

The titles in this series are designed to provide a forum for interpreting, in clear, straightforward language, current issues and trends affecting education. Teachers are invited to share — in their own voice — the insights, wisdom and knowledge they have developed out of their professional experiences.

Submissions for publication are welcomed. Manuscripts and proposals will be reviewed by members of the Pippin Teacher's Library Editorial Advisory Board, chaired by Lee Gunderson, PhD, of the University of British Columbia.

Members of the Editorial Advisory Board are:
Karen Feathers, PhD, of Wayne State University.
Richard McCallum, PhD, of the University of California, Berkeley.
Jon Shapiro, PhD, of the University of British Columbia.
Jan Turbill, MEd, of the University of Wollongong, New South Wales.
David Wray, PhD, of the University of Exeter, England.

Written submissions should be directed to:
The Editorial Director
Pippin Publishing Corporation
85 Ellesmere Road
Suite 232
Toronto, Ontario
Canada
M1R 4B9